D0305443
TH
THE POLYTECHNIC

Barry Maybury

WRITERS' WORKSHOP
Techniques in Creative Writing

B. T. Batsford Ltd
London

By the same author

Creative Writing for Juniors (Batsford)
Wordscapes
Thoughtshapes,
Bandstand,
Bandwagon,
Images (all Oxford University Press)

First published 1979

Printed and bound in Great Britain by
Billing & Sons Ltd, Guildford, London & Worcester
for the Publishers B. T. Batsford Ltd,
4 Fitzhardinge Street, London W1H 0AH

ISBN 0 7134 1557 6

CONTENTS

Acknowledgements

I would like to express my grateful thanks to Joan, Val, and Ruth for help and understanding in preparation of the book, to Brian Rees-Williams for reading the typescript, and especially to students past and present at the North Worcester College, with whom I worked and who made valuable contributions.

Grateful acknowledgement is also due to the authors, proprietors or executors and to the publishers of the poems, extracts and letters reproduced in the book:

Bainbridge, Beryl, Gerald Duckworth & Co. Ltd, and Fontana paperbacks for an extract from *The Bottle Factory Outing*

Beckett, Samuel and Calder and Boyars Ltd for an extract from *Murphy*

Berger, John, Weidenfeld & Nicolson Ltd and Penguin Books Ltd for an extract from *G*

Blishen, Edward and Leon Garfield, Longman Group Ltd and Corgi paperbacks for an extract from *The God Beneath the Sea*

Bownas, Geoffrey and Anthony Thwaite and Penguin Books Ltd for translation of Japanese Haiku from *The Penguin Book of Japanese Verse*

Camus, Albert (Estate of), Stuart Gilbert for the translation, Hamish Hamilton Ltd and Penguin Books Ltd for an extract from *L'Etranger (The Outsider)*

Cirlot, J. E. and Routledge & Kegan Paul Ltd for an extract from *A Dictionary of Symbols*

Cudlip, Hugh and The Bodley Head Ltd for an extract from *Walking on the Water*

Durrell, Lawrence and Faber & Faber Ltd for extracts from *The Alexandrian Quartet*

Dürrenmatt, Friedrich, Walter Wagner as editor and Longman Group Ltd for an extract from *The Playwrights Speak*

Eliot, T. S. (Estate of) and Faber & Faber Ltd for extracts from *Collected Poems, Four Quartets, The Waste Land and Other Poems* and *The Sacred Wood*

Fang, Achilles for translation of Chinese poem from *New Mexican Quarterly*

Finlay, Ian Hamilton and Eugene Goningen and Indiana Press for poems from *Concrete Poetry* and also the *Times Literary Supplement*

Forster, E. M., (Estate of) and Edward Arnold (Publishers) Ltd for an extract from *Aspects of the Novel*

Frost, Robert (Estate of), Jonathan Cape Ltd and Penguin Books Ltd for extracts from *Selected Poems*
Graves, Robert and Cassell & Co. Ltd for "The Legs" and "Welsh Incident" from *Collected Poems*
Greene, Graham, William Heinemann Ltd and Penguin Books Ltd for an extract from *The Power and the Glory*
Guardian newspapers for news items
Hart-Smith, W. and Angus and Robertson (UK) Ltd for "Observation" from *The Unceasing Ground*
Heaney, Seamus and Faber & Faber Ltd for an extract from *Death of a Naturalist*
Heller, Joseph and Corgi paperbacks for an extract from *Catch 22*
Hemingway, Ernest (Estate of) and Jonathan Cape Ltd for an extract from "In Our Time" from *The First 49 Stories*
Hughes, Ted and Faber & Faber Ltd for extracts from "Pike" and "An Otter" from *Lupercal,* "Still Life" from *Wodwo, Gaudete* and *Poetry in the Making*
Johnson, B. S. (Estate of), Secker & Warburg Ltd and Panther Books Ltd for an extract from *Trawl;* and B. S. Johnson, Constable & Co. Ltd and Panther Books Ltd for an extract from *Albert Angelo*
Joyce, James (Estate of), Penguin Books Ltd and Jonathan Cape Ltd (for extracts from *A Portrait of the Artist as a Young Man* and *Stephen Hero*), The Bodley Head Ltd (for extracts from *Ulysses*), and Faber & Faber Ltd (for an extract from *Finnegans Wake*)
Kesey, Ken and Signet Books for an extract from *One Flew over the Cuckoo's Nest*
Kinsale, Paddy for "Imago"
Langer, Susanne and Signet Books for extracts from *Philosophical Sketches*
Lawrence, D. H. (Estate of Mrs Freda Lawrence), William Heinemann Ltd and Penguin Books Ltd for "Terra Incognita" from *Collected Poems* and for an extract from *The Rainbow*
Leavis, F. R. and Cambridge University Press for an extract from *Scrutiny*
Lee, Laurie and The Hogarth Press Ltd for "Day of these Days" from *The Sun my Monument,* and the Hogarth Press Ltd and Penguin Books Ltd for an extract from *Cider with Rosie*
Lennon & McCartney for a line from a song
Loewinsohn, Ron and LeRoi Jones Totem Press for "The Thing

Made Real" from *Watermelons*
London, Jack and Signet Books for an extract from "To Build a Fire" from *The Call of the Wild & Selected Stories*
Lowell, Amy and Houghton Mifflin Company for "Dolphins in Blue Water"
MacCaig, Norman and The Hogarth Press Ltd for "An Ordinary Day" from *Surroundings*
McCullers, Carson, Cresset Press and Penguin Books Ltd for an extract from *The Member of the Wedding*
Morgan, Edwin, and Edinburgh University Press for poems from *The Second Life*
Murdoch, Iris, Chatto & Windus Ltd and Penguin Books Ltd for extracts from *The Sandcastle* and from *A Severed Head*
Orwell, George (Estate of) and Penguin Books Ltd for an extract from *Nineteen Eighty-Four*
Paes, José Paulo and the *Times Literary Supplement* for "Cogito ergo boom"
Pinter, Harold, Walter Wagner as editor and Longman Group Ltd for an extract from *The Playwrights Speak;* and Harold Pinter and Methuen & Co. Ltd for an extract from "Last to Go" from *A Slight Ache and Other Plays*
Plath, Sylvia (Estate of, i.e. Ted Hughes) and Faber & Faber Ltd for extracts from "Sculptor" and "Mirror" from *The Colossus* and *Ariel*
Pearce, Philippa and Oxford University Press for an extract from *Tom's Midnight Garden*
Proust, Marcel (Estate of), C. K. Scott-Moncrieff for the translation and Chatto & Windus Ltd for an extract from *Swann's Way*
Purcell, Victor and Penguin Books Ltd for "The Voice of Sweeney" from *More Comic and Curious Verse*
Richards, I. A. and Routledge & Kegan Paul Ltd for an extract from *Coleridge on Imagination*
Richter, Irma A. and Oxford University Press for an extract from *Selections from the Notebooks of Leonardo da Vinci*
Roberts, Nesta for news items from *The Guardian*
Spring, Howard (Estate of) and Fontana paperbacks for an extract from *Shabby Tiger*
Stallworthy, John and Oxford University Press for an extract from *Between the Lines*
Summerfield, Geoffrey and BBC Publications for an extract from "Windy Boy in a windswept Tree" from *Adventures in English*

Thomas, Dylan (Estate of) and Dent & Sons Ltd for extracts from "Fern Hill", *Under Milk Wood, A Prospect of the Sea, Quite Early One Morning;* Dylan Thomas, Henry Treece, T. H. Jones as editor and Oliver & Boyd for an extract from a letter in *Dylan Thomas;* and Dylan Thomas, Pamela Hansford Johnson, Constantine Fitzgibbon as editor and Dent & Sons Ltd for an extract from a letter in *Selected Letters*

White, Patrick, Jonathan Cape Ltd and Penguin Books Ltd for extracts from *The Tree of Man* and *The Eye of the Storm*

Woolf, Virginia (Estate of), The Hogarth Press Ltd and Penguin Books Ltd for extracts from *Jacob's Room* and *The Common Reader*

Yeats, W. B. (Estate of) and Macmillan Publishers Ltd for extracts from *Collected Poems*

And special thanks to the young writers:

Pamela Spratt and Oxford University Press for her poem on "Hands"

Pat Prentice and Julie Parker for their Haiku, from *Rutland Writers*

Mark Holloway and Workshop Press for "Folded Poem"

Rosemary Kathleen Chandler and William Heinemann Ltd for "As the Mirrors Lie" from *Daily Mirror Children as Writers 4*

Gillian and Hutchinson & Co. Ltd for her poem "A Gardener drinking Tea" from *Young Writers Young Readers*

FOREWORD

It is hoped that this book will be found useful in the upper forms of secondary schools, in colleges of further education, polytechnics and universities, where teachers and lecturers are aiming to promote personal or imaginative writing. It will perhaps also be of value to anyone in the wider public who is interested in creative writing.

The intention behind the book is to offer ideas and techniques which students will find it enjoyable to work at, as part of a particular course in writing or as an extension of their literary studies, or simply to play around with at odd moments when they have a pencil and paper handy.

Experience of working with students suggests that often, when faced with the challenge of writing, students find their imagination freezes; they protest that they have no ideas worth putting down, or they may even be led to claim that they have no imagination. While I sympathize with the teacher who may be tempted to endorse such a claim, I would argue that such a state of affairs is more often apparent than real. What such students need is some interesting lead into an idea, or some approach which will catch their imagination in the way it was seized when they were younger listening to stories, or in the way it is still seized by visual images in film or television. It is my intention to offer suggestions that will do just that.

Clearly, it would be unwise to claim that the material within these pages will always appeal to all students, but it is hoped that—to paraphrase— some of it will appeal some of the time. A lot depends on mood, the prevailing climate of interest, the news, the weather even, as to how we are inclined to an idea. As an example, I am working on a novel at the moment, it is a particularly stormy day, and the storm has found its way into my writing and provided several ideas which are not only to do with the atmosphere in which the characters are operating; I notice that it has influenced the imagery, the words chosen even. I may have to abandon this later, but it has provided a framework in which for the time being I can write. It might have worked differently, of course: the storm might perversely have provided a placid, sunny day for the events to take place in, or it might have driven my principal character into introspection. I don't wish to suggest that we should abandon our creative disposition entirely to the vagaries of the weather or climate, but the influence is so often there, even if we resist it. And so it may be with anything about us: objects, people, animals, buildings. Any or all may affect our mood and our imaginative awareness, but, more interestingly, they may provide us with a source of raw material for our writing. In part, this is what this book is about.

The ideas are arranged in a form I've found it convenient to use with students, but probably any pattern or sequence would do as well. So much depends on the personality of the teacher and the interests of the students. There was no intention to plan a progressive course, though I know some teachers and students are happier if they are working in such a framework. I would hope that teachers might use the book as a source of material that relates to whatever they are engaged in at any particular moment; as an adjunct to other kinds of writing; and as a store of ideas for extending work in other areas, for example in the study of imaginative literature, essay-writing, preparing lessons with children, writing reports, doing work preparatory to examinations in English where students are required to write personally, and so forth. It should also suggest ideas for consideration and discussion in those odd moments at the end of tutorial periods and lessons, when something different or tangential seems appropriate.

The material is arranged in a way that I hope will appeal to a variety of interests and levels of ability. Usually there are developmental suggestions to allow for individual needs, moods or flights of fancy. There are also follow-up suggestions for further reading, for other poems, extracts or stories which the teacher might use in class or the students might be referred to. The book could be used either as a handbook from which the teacher quarries ideas to present to the students, or as a class book which students work with at their own pace and according to their own dispositions. And so the book is addressed to students directly, but also to teachers and lecturers, so that while some of the introductory narrative is such that teachers might like to use it to introduce an idea, the actual suggestions for work are set at a more personal level, sometimes aimed at the student specifically, or at the student through the teacher, and quite often at both. This is in the belief that the work will be more interesting and have more meaning if the teacher is directly involved, trying out the idea himself beforehand or while the students are writing.

For those wishing to plan programmes of work alternative to what is indicated in the list of Contents I suggest the use of the Index and the Thematic Index at the end of the book.

OPENING WORDS

Camus began his novel *L'Etranger*[1] with the sentence:

> Mother died today. Or, maybe, yesterday; I can't be sure.

Few novels begin in such an arresting way. The sentence states a major theme in the book; also it challenges our attitudes and, in doing so, raises important philosophical questions with which the book will be concerned, not as abstract theorizing, but in terms of people and their thoughts and actions.

Quite often a novelist, having written his story, will come back to rewrite the beginning several times, or perhaps even cut it out altogether. It is important to get it right, to make the right kind of impact, perhaps to create the right mood or atmosphere for the story. Here are the opening paragraphs of Graham Greene's *The Power and the Glory:*[2]

> Mr Tench went out to look for his ether cylinder, into the blazing Mexican sun and the bleaching dust. A few vultures looked down from the roof with shabby indifference: he wasn't carrion yet. A faint feeling of rebellion stirred in Mr Tench's heart, and he wrenched up a piece of the road with splintering finger-nails and tossed it feebly towards them. One rose and flapped across the town: over the tiny plaza, over the bust of an ex-president, ex-general, ex-human being, over the two stalls which sold mineral water, towards the river and the sea. It wouldn't find anything there: the sharks looked after the carrion on that side. Mr Tench went on across the plaza.
>
> He said *'Buenos días'* to a man with a gun who sat in a small patch of shade against a wall. But it wasn't like England: the man said nothing at all, just stared malevolently up at Mr Tench, as if he had never had any dealings with the foreigner, as if Mr Tench were not responsible for his two gold bicuspid teeth. Mr Tench went sweating by, past the Treasury which had once been a church, towards the quay. Half-way across he suddenly forgot

[1]Translated as *The Outsider* by Stuart Gilbert (Hamish Hamilton/Penguin)
[2]Heinemann/Penguin

what he had come out for—a glass of mineral water? That was all there was to drink in this prohibition state—except beer, but that was a government monopoly and too expensive except on special occasions. An awful feeling of nausea gripped Mr Tench in the stomach—it couldn't have been mineral water he wanted. Of course his ether cylinder...the boat was in. He had heard its exultant piping while he lay on his bed after lunch. He passed the barbers' and two dentists and came out between a warehouse and the customs on to the river bank.

This is an extremely effective opening, worth discussing in some detail, and students might do this. How would you describe the mood of the piece? Certainly it is sultry, lethargic, and has perhaps a pervasive hopelessness. Nothing seems to matter, noone has any energy, except perhaps to pull a trigger. How is the effect created? Clearly, it is in the words the author chooses, and in what he chooses to notice, in the detail, in fact. The vultures have a "shabby indifference", Mr Tench throws a piece of stone "feebly", it is only a "faint" feeling of rebellion. Another important aspect is the sense of menace, or threat: the man with the gun to whom Mr Tench says good morning just stares "malevolently".

There is a good deal more that might be instanced in the extract which assists the general mood, sets the scene for the events which are to take place. Mr Greene may have worked very hard on this passage, going over it again and again, or it may have come right the first time, as sometimes happens.

Students might like to collect openings to stories which they find interesting or impressive, or perhaps even uninviting, and note briefly why they have these impressions. Below are suggested some books, the beginnings of which have some particular feature worth comment.

A famous popular novelist of the 'thirties and 'forties, Howard Spring, once began a novel with the words, "She flamed along the road like a macaw..."[1]—certainly a very vivid and colourful image. Perhaps you would like to make some story openings of your own, and having made some, choose one and sketch out ways in which you might carry on with the story. Or, better still, write it. Here are some openings contributed by various students:

[1] *Shabby Tiger* (Fontana)

He was riding across the desert on a bicycle/donkey/big dog...
Captain Cathcart stepped out of the capsule onto blue grass...
There was a light at the end of the tunnel...
Exhausted, he crawled onto the sandy beach...
As she knitted the jumper she became aware of a pattern...
"Do yourself a favour—get lost!"...
Summer came and went...
She cried with no sound...
He opened the wallet and found it contained several hundred pounds...
She stopped writing and closed the book...
I begin this journal...
The door closed behind her, leaving her in total darkness...
She was pretty with bright blue eyes, but her head was on the wrong way...
When Tobias emerged from the garden/jungle/pram/circus, his hair was white...
"No, it isn't rabies. It's something else!"...
Fullbright scratched his nose ruminatively...
The fog was thickening...
He lifted the hand, and saw that the third finger was missing...
"By the way," she said, "your soup was poisoned."...
He was walking down the street...

Most of these have some intriguing quality which makes me, at any rate, wonder what might follow. But, of course, a simple statement might be just as effective, depending on what follows. Consider the last item for instance.

But whatever you choose in order to begin your writing, you won't have gone very far before you will encounter interesting problems which must be solved or deferred: Who? Why? What is the explanation? What will the result be? What sort of people are they? etc.

SOME MORE OPENINGS TO CONSIDER

"The sun shone, having no alternative, on nothing new". Samuel Beckett *Murphy* (Calder)

"They're out there". Ken Kesey *One Flew over the Cuckoo's Nest* (Signet)

"It was a bright cold day in April, and the clocks were striking thirteen". George Orwell *Nineteen Eighty-Four* (Penguin)

"It was love at first sight. The first time Yossarian saw the Chaplain he fell madly in love with him". Joseph Heller *Catch 22* (Corgi)

LIMBERING UP

1) FREE ASSOCIATION. Write any associations you can think of in a short period of time, say thirty seconds, for the following:
   stone rose bread sea fire bone time
2) Freely associate any ideas, images, words you can think of, regardless of whether the ideas form complete sentences or even make sense, in connection with any of the following:
   A house stream pub garden graveyard mountain
3) Choose one of the following objects, or an object from your own life or experience, and freely associate in connection with it:
   gold ring comb purse gramophone record thimble
   key coin egg-timer penknife earrings
   paper-weight watch ribbon letters
4) Close your eyes, empty your mind, and then write down any ideas or words that come into it, and freely associate them.
5) Take one of the words in (1)— SEA, for example—and generate as many ideas and images associated with it as you can. Try to think laterally as well as in one particular area. (For example, you might be stuck on the sea*side*, but remember there's also the world beneath the sea, the moods of the sea, shipwreck, untravelled regions, etc.)
6) Now try some formal arrangement of this material. For example, you might simply begin with some phrase such as "The sea is...", and repeat it every few lines. Or, perhaps, end every few lines with some phrase such as "...echoes the sea."
7) Now try an extension of the form, still using "sea" and the images and words you have associated, by finding a rhyme or half-rhyme for the line endings, eg:
   shell bell lull fall full call
   waves raves caves loves moves heaves
   sounding pounding roaring echoing mourning
   murmuring

8) Now try metaphorical forms, eg:
darks of the sea shores of the sea gods of the sea
graves of the sea times of the sea loves of the sea
dreams of the sea bones of the sea jewels of the sea
9) Other metaphor forms:
sea like blood sea like the mind sea like night sea dream
seasword seanight seadead seamoan sea-fire seadeath
sea anger sea light
10) Now try a poem called "A Drowning", or "Sea Death", or "Sea Dream".
11) Now try one on STONE. Here are some images:
lichen-covered ragged gorse-encrusted watching the road below foot-stepped rocky crags grey rocks craggy rocks outcrops mica-flecked mica-glinted frost-glinted diamond-flecked quartz-encrusted quartz-clustered gold of the lichen velvet mossed grey rock shadows the grass heavy with the earth, giving little to the sky bearing the head and weight of the slow afternoon sliding, slides in the winter snow and the footsteps of shepherds the unfathomable obscurity of grey stone
12) Collect poems and extracts from anthologies on or concerned with the sea, rock, etc, and observe how the poets handle these ideas. See, for instance, Ted Hughes' "Still Life"[1], "Relic"[2]; Gerard Manley Hopkins' "The Wreck of the Deutschland" and "The Sea and The Skylark"; Clarence's dream of beneath the sea from *Richard III* (Act I, sc.iii); Lawrence Durrell's description of the rock pool from *Clea* (Appendix p 156). See also p 37 of this book for an extract from Joyce's *Ulysses.*

HANDS I

Look at your hands, explore their contours, lines, texture of the skin. Close your eyes and see them in your imagination—nails, scars, ring, etc.

Close your eyes and think of hands shaping something in metal or

[1]In Ted Hughes *Wodwo* (Faber) [2]In Ted Hughes *Lupercal* (Faber)

wood, hammering or filing, hands tugging, gesturing, soothing, caressing, the hands of a dancer, a doctor operating on a heart, an artist painting, a musician playing the piano, violin, hands applying make-up, tying shoe-laces, undressing, washing up, peeling an apple, etc. Think of hands doing heavy work, heaving, hauling, say on the sails of a boat; hands doing delicate work, say watch-making, painting miniatures. Think of the hands of a particular person, perhaps from some moment in history, signing a treaty for instance, striking a blow; think of a ploughman's hands, blacksmith's hands, Leonardo painting the Mona Lisa, hands of a knight murdering Thomas à Becket, a child's hands, lovers' hands, hands of an old man, hands like...

Make up some images for hands. If you are stuck, simply make a list of hands doing different things, and against them put a word to describe their nature or quality.

Here's a short poem by a twelve-year-old girl:

My hands have been working,
Working very hard,
Now they are hot,
Hot and clammy.
Their colour is pink and black.
Blotches of Black Ink.
They have been working all day long.
Scrubbing teeth, washing faces
Eating breakfast, Writing, –
What could I do
Without my hands?
Practically Nothing.

Pamela Spratt, aged 12[1]

Using any of the above material, or your own ideas, write a piece of free verse or a formal poem under the title "Hands".

Write a piece of prose—an extract from a projected story, say, or a moment from a scenario for a film or TV play—where the interest focuses on the hands of some individual or individuals (serious or comic, as you like).

---

[1]First published in *Bandwagon* (OUP)

FURTHER SUGGESTIONS

1) Look at Dürer's etching of hands. Collect pictures of hands, try to represent what you see in words. Examine the way hands are depicted in paintings.
2) Consider a hand in the act of closing on the controls of a rocket-ship, butt of a revolver, fingers gripping rockface, putting final brush-stroke to painting, etc. Explore detail in this.
3) Write a piece about hands from babyhood to old age.
4) Write a ghost story called "The Hand". (If you are interested, read Guy de Maupassant's story of the same name.)

Here are examples of pieces of writing in class:

> Hands move silently about the room, sunlight flowing over them like water
> Tending the roses, the hands arrange them stem by stem, touching petal and leaf with care
> The hands arrange the music on the piano,
> Open the window and pause on the catch
> Pick up a magazine, restlessly flick the pages...

> Hands clutched the mud, clawed the earth,
> Hoisted, they gripped the stock in fear.
> Hands found the haft of the bayonet,
> Hands deftly locked the blade,
> Hands allowed themselves to move over the mud,
> Hands let go, released, relaxed, hands opened to the stars.

Both pieces are little more than lists, but they both have a mood created by the images and this could be developed. Both items in fact are the first rough drafts of what might turn into poems (For a poet's first drafts see p 165ff. See also p 30.)

SEE extract in Appendix p 166 from John Berger's novel *G.*

Having tried out a piece on hands, try one on feet. See Robert Graves' poem "The Legs" in Appendix, p 167.

IMAGES

By an image I mean anything conceived in the imagination and expressed in verbal terms: "the sculptur'd dead" is an image. The image may be developed, of course, so that it becomes more detailed:

The sculptur'd dead, on each side, seem to freeze,
Emprison'd in black, purgatorial rails:

and, further, so that it becomes an active, moving picture like a movie, as opposed to a still camera:

The sculptur'd dead, on each side, seem to freeze,
Emprison'd in black, purgatorial rails:
Knights, ladies, praying in dumb orat'ries,
He passeth by; and his weak spirit fails
To think how they may ache in icy hoods and mails.[1]

The sensitive reader might even go so far as to claim he not only has a visual image of these statues of the dead, but can even sense the *feel* of the cold stone their forms are encased in.

The image may be, so to speak, an intellectual image, depending for its power to act on us on our ability to grasp intellectually the *function* of the poet's terms, as we may have to grasp the function of an algebraic equation:

My love is of a birth as rare
As 'tis for object, strange and high:
It was begotten by despair
Upon impossibility.[2]

It was "begotten", so the image works in terms of a conceiving, a pregnancy and a birth; but both "despair" and "impossibility" are abstract terms and have to be conceived or engendered in the imagination and the intellect. One might argue that these are not diverse faculties, but only themselves *images* for something we find it very difficult to envisage.

[1]John Keats "The Eve of St. Agnes" [2]Andrew Marvell "The Definition of Love"

Images can derive from any of the senses and appeal to any of the senses—not only the visual. To draw again from the poetry of John Keats, from the same poem, much commented upon for its sensory, if not sensual, appeal:

And still she slept an azure-lidded sleep,
In blanchèd linen, smooth and lavender'd,
While he from forth the closet brought a heap
Of candied apple, quince, and plum, and gourd;
With jellies soother than the creamy curd,
And lucent syrops, tinct with cinnamon;
Manna and dates, in argosy transferr'd
From Fez; and spicèd dainties, every one,
From silken Samarcand to cedar'd Lebanon.

I would suggest that the appeal, apart from the visual, is also to the touch ("blanchèd linen", "smooth and lavender'd"), to the sense of smell ("lavender'd"), to the taste obviously, to a general, almost narcotic awareness, which moves into the sensual.

Of course, as individuals we have different degrees of responsiveness to different sensory appeals: some people remark that for them the sense of smell is the most evocative, others remember taste vividly, and it seems reasonable that we therefore tend to favour one sense above another, and consequently respond better or more readily to one than another, which might account for the differences in student reactions to some poetry. Peter McKeller[1] suggests that Joan of Arc's voices may have been attributable to a particularly potent auditory imagination, and further ponders on the number of unfortunates who have been victimized or even martyred in the past because one aspect of their imagination, one sensory faculty, was more vigorous than was normal. Blake, for example, writes as though he actually saw angels at the dinner table. Elsewhere in a letter he seems to have been fully aware of the way his vision worked:

For double the vision my eyes do see,
And a double vision is always with me.
With my inward eye 'tis an Old Man grey,
With my outward, a Thistle across my way.[2]

[1]Peter McKeller *Imagination and Thinking* (Cohen & West)

[2]From a poem in a letter to Thomas Butts, dated 'Felpham, Nov. 22, 1802'

As I have already noted, images may be developed and sometimes developed elaborately with powerful effect, as in the following passage in which Cleopatra is rapturously recreating her vision of Antony:

Cleopatra: *I dreamt there was an Emperor Antony.*
O such another sleep, that I might see
But such another man!
Dolabella: *If it might please ye –*
Cleo.: *His face was as the heavens, and therein stuck*
A sun and moon, which kept their course, and lighted
The little O, the earth.
Dol.: *Most sovereign creature, –*
Cleo.: *His legs bestrid the ocean, his rear'd arm*
Crested the world: his voice was propertied
As all the tuned spheres, and that to friends:
But when he meant to quail, and shake the orb,
He was as rattling thunder. For his bounty,
There was no winter in 't: an autumn 'twas
That grew the more by reaping: his delights
Were dolphin-like, they show'd his back above
The element they lived in: in his livery
Walk'd crowns and crownets: real realms and islands were
As plates dropp'd from his pocket.
Dol.: *Cleopatra!*
Cleo.: *Think you there was, or might be such a man*
As this I dreamt of?
Dol.: *Gentle madam, no.*[1]

A fascinating, complex passage in which all sorts of ideas are being touched on. Students might like to discuss it.

Sometimes the image, apparently simple, is suddenly made complex, enriched in fact by the addition of another image:

I sang in my chains like the sea[2]

This brief discussion doesn't of course exhaust the subject of imagery. My intention is simply to raise a few questions and attempt a working definition, so that if I suggest students jot down a few images, they will have some ideas about what I mean. Also it may raise a few questions about the nature of imagery which might extend students' interest and promote different kinds of attempts at writing.

[1] Shakespeare *Antony and Cleopatra,* Act V sc.ii

[2] Dylan Thomas "Fern Hill" in *Collected Poems by Dylan Thomas* (Dent)

The discussion will I hope go on, but for the moment I would like to concentrate, simply as an exercise, on a fairly restricted sort of writing, which has an immediate appeal and at least has the merit that it can give immediate pleasure, because of its brevity. (Which is not to say that the form may not be subtle.) I would like to suggest that students attempt some Haiku. Essentially this Japanese verse form has three lines of 5, 7 and 5 syllables. Unless this is considered a challenge that cannot be avoided, I suggest that you simply try a number of three-line poems. The following examples will give some idea of the effectiveness of such images:

An old pond
A frog jumps in –
Sound of water.

Far-off mountain peaks
Reflected in its eyes:
The dragonfly.

In the old man's eyes
The piercing sun
Looks fuddled.

Iron autumn
And all the cold
Windbells tinkling.[1]

And some by young students:

The hustle and bustle
Of the crowded street
Like birds in Autumn
Pat Prentice, 13

The snowflakes, falling one at a time
Floating slowly to the ground;
A white sheet appears.
Julie Parker, 15[2]

[1]Japanese Haiku from *The Penguin Book of Japanese Verse* translated by Geoffrey Bownas and Anthony Thwaite

[2]From *Rutland Writers*

After this, students might like to take some single theme and devise or generate as many images related to it as they can think of, eg:

Walking in the snow
Watching trains
Buses in the rain, trees in the rain, etc
Coffee time
The machine shop
Circus
Piano music
Bird soaring
Leaves falling
Blast furnace at night
Child on a swing
Goldfish
Clock ticking

I'd like to finish this section with a simple poem which I think illustrates the notion of images very obviously and directly. It's by that arch-priestess of what Ezra Pound called *Amygism*, the American poetess Amy Lowell:

Dolphins in Blue Water

Hey! Crackerjack – jump!
Blue water,
Pink water,
Swirl, flick, flitter;
Snout into a wave-trough,
Plunge, curl.
Bow over,
Under,
Razor-cut and tumble.
Roll, turn –
Straight – and shoot at the sky,
All rose-flame drippings.
Down ring,
Drop,
Nose under,
Hoop,
Tail.
Dive,
And gone;

With smooth over-swirlings of blue water,
Oil-smooth cobalt,
Slipping, liquid lapis lazuli,
Emerald shadings,
Tintings of pink and ochre.
Prismatic slidings
Underneath a windy sky.[1]

USE OF THE IMAGINATION I MORNING

I believe it was Virginia Woolf who, on meeting someone, was likely to ask directly, "What have you been doing today?" And if the reply was, "Nothing" (admittedly a fairly standard response), she was likely to follow this up with, "Well, obviously you got out of bed, didn't you?" The point of her remark was presumably that our lives are filled with a constant stream of experience[2] which goes unnoticed, probably because it has become familiar. For instance, one rarely keeps the bit of broken stone or pebble which one might have been fascinated by as a child. The novelty wears off. We say we have no time to "stand and stare", we must get on. We become obsessed with what we have to do next instead of what we are experiencing now, consequently the present escapes us, that sense of time opening out. But, of course, it is possible to cause ourselves to stand and stare, to filter that common experience through the imagination, which is perhaps one of the things that distinguishes the creative artist from the rest of mankind. The process of ignoring our experience is already beginning in childhood. A pupil says, "I didn't do anything yesterday." If that were really true, the child must have been inert—that in itself is a story.

A colleague of mine[3] used to get his pupils writing by asking them to think what it was like to get up on a cold morning, and then taking suggestions from the class, going through each moment of the process of simply getting out of bed. This is a kind of Proustian approach in which one itemizes all the sensations, all that can be

[1]From *Complete Poems* (Houghton Mifflin Company)
[2]See extract on "stream of consciousness" in Appendix p 169, and p 59
[3]Patrick Creber *Sense & Sensitivity* (ULP)

seen or heard, felt, and, perhaps, thought. Students might take this as a starting point: lying in bed, the decision to get out, the room, inertia, the effort, feet on the cold floor, looking out of the window, the frost on the garden or rooftops, fences, etc; sounds muffled, or abrasive, sounds of breakfast things, milk bottles on doorstep, car engines, garage doors, etc. (See Appendix p 170 for extract from Proust's *Swann's Way* in which he describes lying in bed thinking.)

Having gone through the progress of events, students might concentrate on one of these: looking out of the window, cleaning one's teeth, etc, and explore it in as much detail as possible (eg some people clean their teeth in a perfunctory fashion, while for others it is an elaborate ritual which, even on a cold morning, may require some concentration to accomplish). Shaving or making up the face with cosmetics are other rituals that might be examined in detail.

It is relevant here to say something about form—how to use the material, or these ideas. One way would be to put it into the form of a dialogue with one's self, as in the case of Lily Smalls in *Under Milk Wood*. She looks at herself in the shaving glass:

Oh there's a face!
Where did you get that hair from?
Got it from an old tom cat.
Give it back then, love.
Oh there's a perm!

Where you get that nose from, Lily?
Got it from my father, silly.
You've got it on upside down!
Oh there's a conk!

Look at your complexion!
Oh, no you *look.*
Needs a bit of make-up.
Needs a veil.
Oh there's glamour!

Where you get that smile, Lil?
Never mind, girl.
Nobody loves you.
That's what you *think.*

Who is it loves you?
Shan't tell.

Come on, Lily.
Cross your heart then?
Cross my heart.

FIRST VOICE

And very softly, her lips almost touching her reflection she breathes the name and clouds the shaving glass.[1]

Alternatively, your material might be put in the mode of a first-person reflection, as in the Proust extract referred to above, or of a third-person description, the opening of a novel perhaps.

Or students might like to try the narrative form, moving into the interior monologue, as Joyce does in this extract from *Ulysses*[2]. Mr Bloom is up in the morning and thinking about breakfast, and about taking a tray of bread and butter up to his wife, Molly:

> Mr Leopold Bloom ate with relish the inner organs of beasts and fowls. He liked thick giblet soup, nutty gizzards, a stuffed roast heart, liver slices fried with crustcrumbs, fried hencod's roes. Most of all he liked grilled mutton kidneys which gave to his palate a fine tang of faintly scented urine.
>
> Kidneys were in his mind as he moved about the kitchen softly, righting her breakfast things on the humpy tray. Gelid light and air were in the kitchen but out of doors gentle summer morning everywhere. Made him feel a bit peckish.
>
> The coals were reddening.
>
> Another slice of bread and butter: three, four: right. She didn't like her plate full. Right. He turned from the tray, lifted the kettle off the hob and set it sideways on the fire. It sat there, dull and squat, its spout stuck out. Cup of tea soon. Good. Mouth dry. The cat walked stiffly round a leg of the table with tail on high.
>
> – Mkgnao!
>
> – O, there you are, Mr Bloom said, turning from the fire. The cat mewed in answer and stalked again stiffly round a leg of the table, mewing. Just how she stalks over my writingtable. Prr. Scratch my head. Prr.
>
> Mr Bloom watched curiously, kindly, the lithe black form. Clean to see: the gloss of her sleek hide, the white button under the butt of her tail, the green flashing eyes. He bent down to her, his hands on his knees.

---

[1]Dylan Thomas *Under Milk Wood* (Dent) [2]Bodley Head/Penguin

– Milk for the pussens, he said.
– Mrkgnao! the cat cried.

Perhaps Mr Bloom, like the rest of us, might have answered Virginia Woolf's question with the reply, "Nothing". Mr Joyce, his creator, has, so to speak, remembered it all for him. Nothing particularly dramatic, nothing out of the way: he thinks of breakfast, the kidneys he particularly likes, he arranges the tray, strokes the cat. And yet Joyce has made it come alive for us, and in the process shown us the richness of ordinary things (as does Norman MacCaig in his poem "An Ordinary Day" – see p 171).

Students might consider the rich detail of their own ORDINARY experience, and utilize it, use it as raw material for their writing.

THE SHORT STORY

One nice thing about the short story is that you can read it at a sitting in one go, and very often you can write it in the same way. From the point of view of the writing it's nice because you can see the whole thing in perspective, walk around it, so to speak, and see all its features, which is far more difficult to do with a novel. It's also a challenging form for, of course, one can't afford to waste words even for establishing scene or atmosphere. It is important that such detail is absolutely relevant. Often one will naturally use some description or some detail to give the story "place," only to have to excise it later, because it doesn't really do anything very relevant – a painful process, but necessary.

It's difficult to say precisely how one gets ideas for short stories – from a newspaper article, a bit of information overheard in a shop, something half-remembered and suddenly altered by new circumstances. The idea begins to gnaw away at one's imagination, until it's almost necessary to write to find out what happens. Recently somebody told me about a woman returning to a house that she had visited many years before as a young girl and that was now for sale. It was a very large country house, and she managed to get hold of the keys from an estate agent so that she could look it over, which she did, incidentally, unaccompanied. I was curious about the kind of memories she would have in such circumstances, and had to write the story to find out what happened. It turned into a strange past-in-the-present psychological thriller; had I been marginally less schizophrenic at the time, it might have turned out to be an idyllic evocation of a childhood from an earlier age. Henry James describes attending a dinner party where he overheard a conversation about a woman who was having a row with her son over the family house which, along with its contents, he would inherit on his marriage. The woman was afraid that he would pick a wife who would not value the house and its beautiful *objets d'art.* James says he didn't want to know any more; that snatch of conversation had provided him with a seed he had to cultivate in his own way, and from it grew the short novel *The Spoils of Poynton.*[1]

It is probably generally true that the technique employed by a writer is subservient to the idea, that a technique is chosen that seems appropriate for the story. But, of course, that technique itself might well generate material and other, different ideas for the writing. A man sitting bored at a dinner might engage in private fantasies; the technique used might be that of interior monologue, which of course allows him to say (in his head) anything he likes; this itself might create new circumstances: it may well generate new characters, fantasy characters, *personae* perhaps.

While on the subject of fantasies, it might be as well to consider them as the basis for a story, or as the subject of stories. Probably every child writes at sometime or other the kind of adventure which ends "...and then I woke up." We are all Walter Mittys to some extent. It's a good exercise to try and think of a new way of using this device. William Sansom has a very neat story[2] in which a writer admits to his house a chimney-sweep, then goes back to his work and finds himself unable to concentrate. He develops a terrifying conviction that the chimney-sweep is a murderer and that, while he is at the typewriter, the man is murdering his wife. Anyone wanting to find out how a good story-teller handles the idea simply in the quality of his writing might do well to read the story. As a discussion point students might consider how they would handle the idea. (Has he really imagined it all? Is his wife dead and covered with soot? Has he murdered her himself?)

---

[1]Henry James *The Art of The Novel.* [2]"Murder", *Selected Short Stories* (Penguin)

SOME SUGGESTIONS

1) Inside a child's head. Some event, action, or person seen from the child's viewpoint, and perhaps misunderstood or intensified. See "A Message from the Pig-Man" by John Wain.[1] (James said a child gives an extra "turn of the screw". Why? See *The Turn of the Screw* by Henry James.)
2) Begin with an account of someone getting a lift in a car or lorry late at night...
3) In a hotel dining-room, or restaurant, alone at a table, you hear a conversation... (Who are the characters? Who are you? Where is this taking place? Is it significant? Is it to be sinister? Or comic? Or ambiguous?)
4) Return to house, village, town, any place, etc after long absence. Explore possibilities. Alternative: long train journey, your narrator alights at small station. (Night? Day? Deserted? People? Mystery? Is it a dream, a parable, reality?)
5) Examine relationship between adolescent girl and boy.
6) Your narrator is looking out of window of room (flat, office, bed-sit), sees over road at café someone he recognizes. On closer inspection sees that it is himself...

SEE Viewpoint (p 57) and Opening Words (p 11) for other ideas.

SOME SUGGESTED READING

Dorothy Parker "But the One on the Right" in *Points of View* Ed. James Moffatt and Kenneth R. McElheny (Mentor Books)
Daniel Keys "Flowers for Algernon" in *Points of View*
William Carlos Williams "The Use of Force" in *Points of View*
Bernard Malamud "The Prison" in *Points of View*
John Wain "A Message from the Pig-Man" in *Short Stories of Our Time* Ed. Douglas R. Barnes, MA (Harrap's Modern English Series)
Doris Lessing "Through the Tunnel" in *Short Stories of Our Time*
Alan Sillitoe "Uncle Ernest" in *Short Stories of Our Time*
D. H. Lawrence "The Blind Man" in *England My England* (Penguin)

---

[1]In *Short Stories of Our Time* Ed. Douglas R. Barnes, MA (Harrap's Modern English Series).

Jack London "To Build a Fire" in *The Call of the Wild And Selected Stories* (Signet)
Richard Hughes "A Night at a Cottage" in *Aspects of the Short Story* (Murray)
James Joyce "Araby" in *Dubliners*
Angus Wilson "Raspberry Jam" in *The Wrong Set* (Penguin)

COSTUME

Sometimes in a story we need to describe a character's dress and we need particular words which do not necessarily come to hand. This is not to say that to describe a character simply as "dressed in casual clothes" might not in some circumstances be the most appropriate way. To describe his dress down to the last waistcoat button, as Virginia Woolf observed was done of some nineteenth-century novel characters, is not always needful. Nevertheless, if it is important, for some detail of the story, to describe the clothes, it is obviously helpful to have some relevant words to hand. What do you call that kind of jacket which hussars used to wear suspended from the shoulder? Or that long coat coachmen used to wear on all those Dickensian coach journeys? Or the high-necked blouse Edwardian ladies used to favour?

In temporary defiance of Mrs Woolf's maxim try to describe a character down to his last button—comic or serious, in period or contemporary dress. Then, whichever you have tried, attempt a different one.

See what you can find out about the following:

dolman sleeve	bolero
leghorn hat	court shoe
pelisse	hobble skirt
Norfolk jacket	snood
chesterfield (overcoat)	cloche (hat)
Oxford bags	caul

Jot down some more—any you can think of.

What are the following materials? Describe them. Perhaps turn it into a quiz.

watered silk
damascene
cerise
white piqué
lamé
gingham
chenille
flounces
revers
yoke
alpaca
moleskin
cashmere
taffeta
velour
vicuña
mohair
aigrette
corsage
boa
diamanté

When you feel totally familiar with these and any other terms you come across, try to describe a party, say, or a scene in a room, in terms of the clothes people are wearing. Imagine for example that the scene is described from the viewpoint of a dress-designing observer: "Mrs Fanworth, all crêpe-de-chine and georgette, fluttered across the room like a bedraggled bird of paradise and engaged little Miss Mouse primly rigged in tight gingham in predatory conversation..." etc.

Select and discuss some favourite descriptions from novels, etc. Note the use Dickens, for instance, makes of dress; also Jane Austen.

Imagine you wander into another time dimension where famous people from different periods in history are moving about reading, talking, drinking, etc. Describe the scene, paying particular attention to their clothes.

A fancy dress or carnival scene. Describe it as a fashion journalist might, then use this to begin a story.

SEE Doreen Yarwood *English Costume from The Second Century BC to the Present Day* (Batsford) and *The Encyclopaedia of World Costume* (Batsford)

HANDS II

The earlier section on Hands (see p 15) was an attempt to invite students to consider the importance of hands in the life of a human being. The present section is a second look at hands from the viewpoint of description, the way we react to the disposition of people's hands in reality or as described in words on the page. The hands themselves may tell a story. Years ago, so long ago I have forgotten the source, there was a report in a newspaper of an interview with some London street-walkers. One girl was described as having "the calloused hands of a ragpicker". I don't know now quite what the reporter meant by a ragpicker, but the image of the hands seemed then, and still does, a powerful one. Now I think perhaps it tells me a little more about the reporter than the girl; but that apart, the image still seems evocative. Another image I have retained is from a poem called "Sculptor" by Sylvia Plath,[1] in which she describes the sculptor's hands moving over the marble "priestlier than priest's hands". Sometimes in a novel a writer will reinforce the picture of his character by a recurring reference: "Elizabeth's claw...a hand without softness...sharp-pointed silver nails...Elizabeth's clawlike fingers...the clutching ugly hand..." etc. Throughout a book this might help to build up a picture of the character which might be an interesting or nagging sidelight on the personality, or it might be a clue to something significant in the story which only emerges in the dénouement. The above extract is from a novel in which I hoped to convey an aspect of Elizabeth's character which was greedy, clutching, etc. In Patrick White's *The Tree of Man*[2] hands are described again and again:

> 'If this man's hands are not honest,' she said...
>
> The bones of his hand were his, and could better express the poem that was locked inside him and that would never otherwise be released. His hand knew stone and iron, and was familiar with the least shudder of wood. It trembled a little, however, learning the language of flesh...
>
> and the dirt of manual labour was shameful in his hands....
>
> Even her hands at times, he felt, are distant....
>
> The woman watched the man. She did not feel he was resentful of her. He was absorbed in what he was doing. He had flowed away from her into his hands. These had forgotten they had ever touched her it appeared....

All of this incidental material helps to complete the intimate, *unspoken* world of the lives of the two main characters, as well as giving a strong sense of moment, of reality.

Here are some random images of hands which students might like to consider, add to, modify, develop or use in writing. By *modify* I'm thinking that some words or phrases might be altered by substituting

---

[1]In Sylvia Plath *The Colossus* (Faber) [2]Jonathan Cape/Penguin

other words or other forms of expression, eg: Judith's "long elegant hands" might become: hands like porcelain; elegant finger bones of porcelain...; hands of great delicacy, subtly adjusting a collar...; cold porcelain hands, etc. In other words, I am suggesting a little exercise in image-building. Of course, if you were writing a story you'd work at the language that more relevantly expressed what you wanted to say about a person or situation. Here are some examples:

short thick fleshy fingers, black-haired, deeply creased...
hands languidly resting on the table...
hand hanging loosely over the arm of a chair...
fingers splayed over a thigh...
opening out hands in a gesture of uncertainty...
removing some strands of fine hair from her face...
flicking out a hand like some small white bird...
fingers bloated, purple...
riffling her fingers on her shoulder...
she massaged the nape of her neck with one thin hand...
licking his fingers, greasy from the food...
the butts of her fingers, palps of fingers, fingers tightly interlocked...
tracing a word in the air with her fingers...
ancient arthritic hands...
blue-veined and yellow-nailed...

1) Students might notice people's hands and consider ways of describing them.
2) In reading keep an eye open for the way in which writers use images of hands, and the words they choose in order to do this.

SEE Hemingway *The Old Man and The Sea*, and also Appendix p 166.

REMINISCENCE OF CHILDHOOD

"The memories of childhood," says Dylan Thomas, "have no order, and no end." [1] For most of us I suspect that the memories of childhood are the most niggling, pleasurable, disturbing, in fact the most potent memories we carry about with us. If you ask a group of adults to jot down moments from their lives, moments that just occur to them randomly, a large proportion of such memories always seem to derive from childhood. And writers themselves seem irresistibly drawn back to re-explore their own childhood, sometimes in the guise of fiction, sometimes in straight autobiography: Dickens reliving his harrowing experiences in the blacking factory in *David Copperfield;* Joyce trying to re-create the very earliest memories of childhood in *A Portrait of the Artist as a Young Man*[2]*:*

> Once upon a time and a very good time it was there was a moocow coming down along the road and this moocow that was coming down along the road met a nicens little boy named baby tuckoo...
>
> His father told him that story: his father looked at him through a glass: he had a hairy face.
>
> He was baby tuckoo...

Dylan Thomas writing about his Christmases full of aunts and sleeping uncles, walnuts, painting-books, walking in the snow and carol-singing at a house from which all living things seem to have departed except a wizened, dried-up old voice; Laurie Lee discovering water (see p 35); or Seamus Heaney remembering the curiously repulsive fascination for frogspawn:

> *But best of all was the warm thick slobber*
> *Of frogspawn that grew like clotted water*
> *In the shade of the banks. Here, every Spring*
> *I would fill jampotfuls of the jellied*
> *Specks to range on window-sills at home,*
> *On shelves at school, and wait and watch until*
> *The fattening dots burst into nimble-*

---

[1] "Reminiscences of Childhood" (Second Version) in *Quite Early One Morning* (Dent)
[2] Jonathan Cape/Penguin

Swimming tadpoles. Miss Walls would tell us how
The daddy frog was called a bullfrog
And how he croaked and how the mammy frog
Laid hundreds of little eggs and this was
Frogspawn.[1]

Here are some more items chosen from work with students:

Stealing a penny
First day at school
Hanging on the backs of lorries
Pancake day
Visiting an old lady in a large house
A den
Fishing for roach

Students are asked to write out some of their own childhood memories, perhaps selecting one or two and concentrating on the close detail of the experience. Geoffrey Summerfield has a poem in which he describes a boy climbing a tree of which the following is an extract:

The twisted branches lunged and lurched,
His body curved, twisted, he arched
His legs and gripped the bark
Between his ankles.
The crust of bark
Sharp as glasspaper
And rough with wrinkles
Grazed his skin
And raised the raw red flesh
And crazed his mind
With fear of breaking.[1]

Students may have similar images in their own experience, but may be uncertain how to begin. Here are some possible openers:

I remember a tree...
In those days the only trees I knew...
The knotted sharpness of the flaking bark...
The sky opened out...
Below was nothing but the density of leaves...
The day was blotted out with green...

---

[1]From *Death of a Naturalist* (Faber)

[1]From "Windy Boy in a Windswept Tree" *Adventures in English* (BBC)

Some students will be content to leave this at one fragment of writing, others might feel compelled to develop it, or add other experiences to it, building up notes for an autobiography.

OTHER SOURCES OF MATERIAL

D. H. Lawrence *Sons and Lovers* (early chapters) (Penguin) (see particularly pp 24ff, 82ff, 120ff)
James Kirkup *Only Child* (Cape)
Bill Naughton *One Small Boy* (Panther)
Dylan Thomas *Quite Early One Morning* (Dent)

WATER

> The scullery was a mine of all the minerals of living. Here I discovered water—a very different element from the green crawling scum that stank in the garden tub. You could pump it in pure blue gulps out of the ground, you could swing on the pump handle and it came out sparkling like liquid sky. And it broke and ran and shone on the tiled floor, or quivered in a jug, or weighted your clothes with cold. You could drink it, draw with it, froth it with soap, swim beetles across it, or fly it in bubbles in the air. You could put your head in it, and open your eyes, and see the sides of the bucket buckle, and hear your caught breath roar, and work your mouth like a fish, and smell the lime from the ground. Substance of magic—which you could tear or wear, confine or scatter, or send down holes, but never burn or break or destroy.[1]

Water exerts a powerful influence on our imaginations from the first time we play with it in the scullery, like Laurie Lee, swim in it in the ocean, walk along the canal or river as a child, paddle in a stream. Many if not most people find themselves drawn towards water, sometimes dangerously, to peer into it, ruminate on its mysteries, or simply to ponder on the kind of life it contains. Here's an extract from Ted Hughes' poem "Pike"[2] in which he recalls a pond which still lingers darkly, evocatively in his imagination:

[1]From Laurie Lee *Cider with Rosie* (Hogarth Press/Penguin) [2]From *Lupercal* (Faber)

A pond I fished, fifty yards across,
Whose lilies and muscular tench
Had outlasted every visible stone
Of the monastery that planted them –

Stilled legendary depth:
It was as deep as England. It held
Pike too immense to stir, so immense and old
That past nightfall I dared not cast

But silently cast and fished
With the hair frozen on my head
For what might move, for what eye might move.

There is something particularly mysterious, daunting perhaps, about the obsidian darkness of water surface at night, nevertheless curiously compelling.

Some hate it, some find it a lure; it can be placid, violent, sensuous, abrasive; it is the primeval source of life; we all depend on it and in fact are mainly composed of it. It can so easily destroy and readily consume, and many human beings have a life-long love affair with it.

Consider its manifestations, uses, symbolic associations: rain, the sea, baptism, sacred rivers, source of life, storms, etc. Discuss and note down any ideas, memories, poems, stories, myths, that relate to water, rain or the sea.

This might provide you with material for a poem, or you might like to fasten on to one particular aspect of it: rain falling on a garden, sea breaking over rocks, a river, etc.

Another approach is to settle, say, on the effects of rain: in gutters, on window panes, concentric circles in pools, rain in a forest, on rooftops, smell of wet wool, clothes in school, etc.

Think of words and expressions associated with water: globule, blob, gouts of rain, mass of water, sleet, mizzle, drizzle.

You might find it appealing to write a paragraph using any material you like, and trying for effects with descriptive words, or words suggestive of the sounds or quality of water, as Joyce does in this passage from *Ulysses*[1] where Stephen is walking along the shore at Sandymount, moodily introspective, and thinking of the sounds of water in little pools, and the sounds of the sea:

---

[1]Bodley Head/Penguin

> Listen: a fourworded wavespeech: seesoo, hrss, rsseeiss, ooos. Vehement breath of waters amid seasnakes, rearing horses, rocks. In cups of rocks it slops, flop, slop, slap: bounded in barrels. And, spent, its speech ceases. It flows purling, widely flowing, floating foampool, flower unfurling.

SEE section on Rain p 87ff

MUSIC

Debussy "La mer", "Jardins sous la pluie", "Reflets dans l'eau", "La cathédrale engloutie"
Sibelius "Oceanides", *The Swan of Tuonela*
Ravel "Jeux d'eau"
Dvorák "The Water Goblin"
Britten "Sea Pictures" from *Peter Grimes*
Respighi *Fountains of Rome*
Smetana *Vltava*
Liszt "Les jeux d'eaux à la Ville D'Este"

DESCRIBING A ROOM

Describe a room you know well. Afterwards look over the way you have described it. Is it an inventory, a list of objects in the room? Have you found the precise words to describe the features of the room, its furniture, objects and appointments? Or have you made use of periphrasis ("a lot of valuable pieces of furniture of some antique value or interest...") which of course might be effective in some circumstances? In his memoirs[1] Hugh Cudlip gave a brief account of Cecil King's room:

> The room was graced by two Ghiordes Anatolian family prayer-mats, one antique Kermanshah carpet, with a tree bird and foliage design in gold and green, some Chippendale mahogany armchairs, a Hepplewhite wing chair with carved scroll legs upholstered in green silk damask, and a Stuart period oak-panelled side-board. The *objets d'art* included an eighteenth-century bracket clock and gold-splashed bronze bowls....

[1] Hugh Cudlip *Walking on the Water* (Bodley Head)

> A visitor hijacked to the place would assume at first glance that he was at the country retreat of a cultured aristocrat, a former viceroy….

Certainly a room tells you a good deal about the person who lives in it, and in the description of this room there's a strong exotic flavour conveyed by the sound and form of the words, whether or not you happen to know what a Kermanshah carpet or a Ghiordes Anatolian prayer-mat is.

Find other descriptions of rooms, compare them and consider the effect the description has in relation to the characters or the story. For example, on the first page of her novel *The Sandcastle*[1] Iris Murdoch has a description of the Mors' dining-room, which takes the reader out of the small confined place to wider horizons:

> They seated themselves at the table at opposite ends. The dining-room was tiny. The furniture was large and glossy. The casement windows were open as wide as they could go upon the hot dry afternoon. They revealed a short front garden and a hedge of golden privet curling limply in the fierce heat. Beyond the garden lay the road where the neat semi-detached houses faced each other like mirror images. The housing estate was a recent one, modern in design and very solidly built. Above the red-tiled roofs, and over the drooping foliage of the trees there rose high into the soft midsummer haze the neo-Gothic tower of St Bride's School where Mor was a housemaster. It was a cold lunch.

A good deal of the frustrations of Mrs Mor and her effect on her husband are encapsulated here in this description of the dining-room, the garden, its relation to other similar gardens and houses, and the world beyond, which is the world in which they live.

Consider plays in which the action takes place in one room, and the importance of the décor, objects in the room, etc, to the nature of the play (eg John Osborne's *Look Back in Anger,*[2] Harold Pinter's *The Caretaker,*[3] Jean-Paul Sartre's *In Camera*[4]*).*

Consider the significance of certain words or kinds of furniture, drapes, etc, in conveying a sense of a room:

1) imitation leather chairs, tubular steel furniture, oatmeal tweed curtains, a black ceiling, an abstract painting on the wall, golden cushions

---

[1]Chatto & Windus/Penguin
[2]Faber [3]Faber [4]Translation of *Huis Clos* in *Three European Plays* (Penguin)

2) reproduction tudor furniture covered in chintz, woollen tufted half-moon rug on the hearth, brasses on hearth, copper beaten companion set, plaster geese in flight above fireplace, leather pouffe, gilt wicker ottoman with green damask stuffed seat
3) bodged rug on hearth, cast-iron kettle spitting on hob, Dutch oven in front of fire-grate, stranger fluttering on bars, anaglypta square by door, stained and varnished cupboard doors, veneered side-board on which a black marble ormolu clock, in the window a dying fern, brass fender and matching fire-tongs

Students might make a collection of such images or individual words which seem to locate a particular room and ambience.

Describe a room and a suitable character who inhabits it.

Imagine a detective or agent of some kind entering a room. What could be deduced about its occupant from the furniture and contents? Try to build up a picture of the person from the room.

Write a short story called "The Room".

SEE Doreen Yarwood *The English Home* (Batsford)

FIRE

According to the Greek myth, Prometheus stole fire from the gods. The Olympian legend has Prometheus employed by Zeus to make men out of mud and water, and in pity on them stealing fire from heaven to make them live. For this he was chained to a rock where an eagle gnawed his liver each day; at night it was renewed. Eventually Prometheus was released by Hercules. To counterbalance the life men had received, Zeus sent Pandora with her box of miseries.

Fire is often represented by a salamander which is supposed to live in the flames without burning. The Phoenix at the end of its appointed time flies to Arabia where, after building a nest of spices, it consumes itself in flames and is regenerated from the fire. Heraclitus taught that all things are resolved in fire and transmuted by it. For primitive peoples fire is the demiurge, the primeval agent which created the world, emanating from the sun. In Alchemy it is associated with light and also with gold.

Like water, fire easily takes hold of the imagination; indeed, we talk of "firing the imagination". Many of our metaphors suggesting vitality, power, energy, vigorous life, desire, passion, creativity, use the image of flames:

I flam'd amazement:

says Ariel in *The Tempest*.[1] Robert Frost neatly sums it up in his epigrammatic poem "Fire and Ice":

Some say the world will end in fire,
Some say in ice.
From what I've tasted of desire
I hold with those who favour fire.[2]

Students might begin by discussing the metaphors and images we use in connection with fire, the occurrence of fire or works associated with it in poetry—note, for example, the high incidence of such images in Shakespeare. A cursory examination of a dictionary of quotations, *Brewer's Dictionary of Phrase and Fable,* etc, will reveal many interesting examples.

Consider any powerful evocations or manifestations of fire in reality, or in art, literature, folk-lore, or music, eg forest fires, Wotan's Fire Music in Wagner's *Die Walkurie,* a blast furnace, Milton's "adamantine chains and penal fire" at the beginning of *Paradise Lost,* the firestorms caused by the bombing of Cologne and other cities at the end of the Second World War, the Great Fire of London...

Use any of this material or different material for the draft of a poem, or story, or descriptive passage on the theme of fire. Some students might like to use words and images associated with fire in the form of a typographical, or "Shaped" poem (See p 127 also p 135).

Write a short story about some children playing with fire, or about a house on fire.

Write a fantasy about the conflagration in the halls of the gods, or retell the story of Prometheus, or write an extract from an SF story involving fire.

SOME FURTHER EXAMPLES

"There Will Come Soft Rain" in *The Silver Locusts* Ray Bradbury (Panther)

Farenheit 451 Ray Bradbury (Corgi)

Lord of the Flies William Golding (Faber) (p 41ff)

The Tree of Man Patrick White (Penguin) (p 169ff)

---

[1]Act I sc. i l.198 [2]In *Selected Poems* (Penguin), first published by Cape

"The Firebird" in *Russian Tales & Legends* (Oxford)
"That Nature is a Heraclitean Fire" Gerard Manley Hopkins

MUSIC
Falla, Ritual Fire Dance from *El Amor Brujo*
Liszt Symphonic poem *Prometheus*
Stravinsky *The Firebird*

LIGHT

How do you create an impression of the light? The subtle changes of light on a summer afternoon, the glaring intensity of light in the desert, the peculiar quality of light in a place like, for example, Venice, the strange, dubious light of a late afternoon in November, the splashes of light on walls and windows in a car's headlights, the riffling patinas of light on a lake, light fractured in the rain, rinsed by the rain? It all depends on the purpose. It may be that you simply need to convey the information in a story, say, that it is late afternoon when the light is fading, so that the witness to a crime may be mistaken; or it may be that you want to evoke a particular atmosphere (somebody's feelings, perhaps, or mood) and you choose light as the vehicle. Like any other kind of sensory impression, of course, light will find a more immediate response in some than in others. Some people only notice if it is day or night, others detect subtle changes in the effect of the light—just as some people have a strong visual rather than auditory imagination. One must assume that somebody like Beethoven or Joan of Arc had a very strong auditory imagination.[1]

However this may be, the challenge of describing light is one worth taking up because it is so subtle and elusive a task. So let's begin with a fairly accessible example: a sunny afternoon. Light filtering through the leaves of trees, shrubs, onto—what? Grass, water, a brick wall, stone wall, gate, pavement? Suppose the intention is to create a sense of atmosphere, a moment suspended in time, a quiet afternoon, lazy, perhaps, with a sense of past time recalled, echoing in the memory; the light still, or fluttering, begins to dance, there

[1]See p 19

are splashes of light on the path, a wall is saturated with light, a fragile light brushes the door, dabs of light, traceries of light, arabesques of light, furls, fronds, sun splashes, drenches, floods windows…

The suggestion implicit in the dots is that you develop and extend these ideas, perhaps just playing with the words in different collocations, or arranging them in some kind of pattern, or putting them together in sentences, or using the ideas to generate word groupings of your own.

Try the same thing on a DULL DAY or RAINY DAY or concentrate on some particular place, so that you evoke the special quality of the light, eg the mote-laden beams through the tin roof of an old factory, slabs of light in an estate, light in a cathedral or church…

Collect examples of images or passages from the work of other writers and discuss them. Here are a few examples:

> The heaventree of stars hung about with humid nightblue fruit
>
> James Joyce *Ulysses* (Bodley Head/Penguin)

> *Look at the stars! look, look up at the skies!*
> *O look at all the fire-folk sitting in the air!*
> *The bright boroughs, the circle-citadels there!*
> *Down in dim woods the diamond delves! the elves'-eyes!*
> *The grey lawns cold where gold, where quickgold lies!*
> *Wind-beat whitebeam! airy abeles set on a flare!*
> *Flake-doves sent floating forth at a farmyard scare!*
>
> Gerard Manley Hopkins "The Starlight Night"

Incidentally, there is almost certainly reference here to the northern myth of the dwarfs who delved in the earth for treasure, the "fire-dwarfs" who made a necklace for the goddess Freya (now in the heavens as the Seven Sisters) and who appear in the folk tale of *Snow White and the Seven Dwarfs*.

> London was misty with a golden sun-pierced mist in which buildings hung as insubstantial soaring presences. The beautiful dear city, muted and softened, half concealed in floating and slightly shifting clouds, seemed a city in the air, outlined in blurred dashes of grey and brown…
>
> Iris Murdoch *A Severed Head* (Chatto & Windus/Penguin)

Landscape-tones: brown to bronze, steep skyline, low cloud, pearl ground with shadowed oyster and violet reflections. The lion-dust of desert: prophets' tombs turned to zinc and copper at sunset on the ancient lake. Its huge sand-faults like watermarks from the air; green and citron giving to gunmetal, to a single plum-dark sail, moist, palpitant: sticky-winged nymph....Mareotis under a sky of hot lilac.

Lawrence Durrell *Balthazar* (Faber)

Now and then a car came swishing up the road; light splashed over the windows like a deluge of water and drained away instantly...

Beryl Bainbridge *The Bottle Factory Outing*
(Gerald Duckworth/Fontana)

SEE ALSO

Notebooks of G. M. Hopkins, extracts of which appear in *Gerard Manley Hopkins Poems and Prose* Selected by W. H. Gardner (Penguin) (see also p 63)

John Berger *G* (Penguin)

Patrick White *The Eye of the Storm* (Penguin)

OTHER SUGGESTIONS

1) Look up myth of Phaeton and the Horses of the Sun, or Aurora and Tithonus (see Tennyson's poem *Tithonus).* Use the material in a poem or series of images.
2) Look at some paintings such as those by Rembrandt or De La Tour for example, and describe what you see, as for a scene in a book or a story.
3) Give an account of astronauts stepping onto moon, or some imagined planet, as part of SF story in which the light is different, strange, or plays some important part. (Consider the implications of infra-red light.)
4) Describe a visit to house of old person in which the light sets the scene or provides the setting.
5) In your notebook keep a record of impressions of the light. (Refer to the extract from Durrell's *Balthazar* above.)
6) Collect some words and ideas for ways to describe or convey the impression of light. For example, in the preceding extracts notice: "muted", "insubstantial", "blurred", "pearl", etc. Apart from actual words for light, such as lucent, lustrous, opaque, scintillating, etc, lots of expressions are effective when drawn from other senses *(tones,* softened, etc).

MIRRORS

In symbolism the mirror sometimes represents the imagination which depicts the external world. The mirror is often seen as ambivalent since it both reflects images and in some way absorbs them, contains them. According to Cirlot,[1]

> At times it [that is, mirror in folklore] takes the mythic form of a door through which the soul may free itself, 'passing' to the other side.

And there is, of course, the tradition of covering a mirror or turning it to the wall when someone dies, because the soul has passed through it. In his famous film *Orphée,* a modern treatment of the Orpheus and Eurydice myth, Cocteau has Orpheus returning without Eurydice from the underworld back into the world, through a mirror into a room. But apart from in the world of symbolism, mirror images play a large part in our lives: reflections in looking-glass, shop window, pool, someone else's eyes. Make a note of any kind of reflection you can think of. Jot down any stories you can think of involving reflections (eg Narcissus who fell in love with his own image, and, unable to possess it, pined with grief and frustration until he killed himself with a dagger. From the blood which fell to the earth the flower grew. It is interesting that the seer Tiresias prophesied that Narcissus would live to a ripe old age provided he never came to *know* himself).

Other ideas: distorting mirrors in fairgrounds (think of the impression of menace this can give, used to sinister effect in a number of films); the continuous reflection syndrome (looking into a mirror, looking into a mirror, to infinity—most children have done this at some time with a couple of looking-glasses); stepping through a mirror *(Alice Through the Looking-Glass,* for example—would you walk into another world, another time, a different dimension, a different level of the imagination?); looking into a mirror which gives back no reflection (implications? Ghosts are supposed to give back no reflection as they are supposed to cast no shadow); women and mirrors, beauty in a mirror (Snow White story)—the present face is

[1] J. E. Cirlot *A Dictionary of Symbols* (Routledge and Kegan Paul)

the same but each day the glass gives back the past and something of the future, the time passing. Consider the silent, unmoving, complaisant truth-telling of the glass, obdurate, relentless, a kind of reprisal against vanity; the manifestation of the eternal moment; the palpable illusion—into the glass of the present walks the future, stilled by the present, the future is arrested. Here is a poem by Sylvia Plath called "Mirror"[1] which seems to be about this almost mystical relationship we have with mirrors:

I am silver and exact. I have no preconceptions.
Whatever I see I swallow immediately
Just as it is, unmisted by love or dislike.
I am not cruel, only truthful—
The eye of a little god, four-cornered.
Most of the time I meditate on the opposite wall.
It is pink, with speckles. I have looked at it so long
I think it is part of my heart. But it flickers.
Faces and darkness separate us over and over.

Now I am a lake. A woman bends over me,
Searching my reaches for what she really is.
Then she turns to those liars, the candles or the moon.
I see her back, and reflect it faithfully.
She rewards me with tears and an agitation of hands.
I am important to her. She comes and goes.
Each morning it is her face that replaces the darkness.
In me she has drowned a young girl, and in me an old woman
Rises toward her day after day, like a terrible fish.

Discuss the poem and its implications.

Consider the child discovering the mirror, contemplating the opposite reflection of someone he knows such as a mother, etc.

Jot down some mirror words: glance, light, glint, gaze, lucid, etc. Then make these into images.

Some other or related ideas:

Mirror of the past—remembrance of earlier selves
What the future might return from the mirror
Walking through mirror as child

---

[1] From Sylvia Plath *Ariel* (Faber)

The mirror's surface
The mirror's viewpoint
The wrong side of the face

Some images linked into what might be the first draft of a poem:

> The other side of the mirror is the dark side of the soul
> Only when the night comes do the certainties of death
> Dissolve in the mirror's surface
> The pool of light is resolved
> By the drift of time.
> An ice-picture waiting in the stillness of an empty
> room.
> Mirror, mirror of the soul
> Which is the realest of them all
> Those several selves
> Each day dissolves.

Use any of the above ideas or material and arrange or develop them in the form of a poem (free verse, alternating verses, stanzas, a concrete poem), or a short story, or a sound play for tape.

One student suggested a looking-glass in a station waiting-room (before they were all modernized). Obviously, the glass can see certain things, in some respects its vision is limited. Imagine the stories it might tell, or which, so to speak, might be lodged in its confines. The same thing might apply to a mirror in an old house or hotel room. Think of the successive occupants. Suppose, for instance, you could look into the mirror and see past events—lovers, a murder, a mystery, etc. Suppose the mirror "took over", ie controlled the behaviour of the present tenants...

Try a modern version of the Narcissus story, or the Snow White and wicked Queen story, or any story from folk-lore involving a mirror—as a sound play, story, scenario for a film.

Plan a mime, or drama, or ballet sequence involving a mirror, two or three characters with masks. The masks might be used to represent the "selves" behind the mirror frame, etc. Suppose, for example, it is to be a movement sequence and the two lovers see other (more dangerous, frightening, etc) selves. Would these "selves" take over the "real" characters, or try to, would they be rejected, etc? Imagine it as a dance. What music would you use?

Auden says "mirrors are lonely". Consider implications of this and use it as starting point for some writing.

OTHER POEMS, EXTRACTS, ETC
T. S. Eliot Game of Chess from *The Waste Land* (Faber)
Shakespeare Richard with his glass *Richard II* Act IV l. 276-291
Carson McCullers *The Member of the Wedding* (Penguin) (See p 163)
Rosemary K. Chandler "As the Mirrors Lie" *Daily Mirror Children As Writers* (Heinemann) (See p 158)

FOG

Fog is one of those features of weather, like rain on a garden when we look out at it from the inside of a warm room, which tends to make us inwardlooking, possibly because it seems to isolate us, to insulate us from the world, as much as it visually obscures the world about us. What I recall most vividly from childhood about the fog is that the lights would go on early in the afternoon in school and we would be sent home before the normal finishing time. Sometimes we found our way to school with difficulty in the swirling fog of the morning to discover that only half the class had arrived. Then the teacher put a more than usual amount of coke into the stove in the old classroom and it became a special kind of day—quiet, private, in which the teacher's voice alone in a succession of stories or subdued instructions disturbed the muffled silence of our activities. The classroom then seemed very large and very high, and over our milk we huddled within ourselves, and waited to see what would happen next—the headmaster to enter and confer about the thickening fog, our teacher to put on her coat in the classroom (a sure sign of something untoward), whispered news that the world had finally stopped, as though we didn't already know that. All day we waited for the something that was the message that we were to leave school early. And all day we peered out of the window at the enveloping greyness that reduced street lamps to minute sparkling points and shrunk the world to this warm and muted, echoing room. And then at last the headmaster would appear in the doorway and nod significantly to our teacher and we waited like predatory cats, observing each nuance of her expression before she tidied away her paper so slowly and deliberately into the tall desk, turned to us, paused, maintaining the suspense she had so carefully engendered, and announced that we should put away our books which for half an hour we had been pretending to read while stealing furtive glances at our teacher's next movement. We "sat up straight", silently raised our hinged seats which we normally banged up with a flourish, said our prayers and scuffled out, mufflered, peering slit-eyed, hands plunged deep into trousers' pockets, and slid into the deadening mist where shapes loomed like insubstantial ghosts anxious to dissolve themselves along with cars, pillar-boxes and trees into the clinging ubiquitous grey.

I've tried at some length to recapture my recollections, because fog is not an easy thing to describe and I felt I ought to have a go at it myself. I wouldn't claim any literary merit for my paragraph, but there are one or two things in it worth pointing out. It's rather about the effect the fog had on our day than about the fog itself. I suppose I was cheating a little, hoping I would get some support for my account by touching a few nostalgic chords—the evocation of the old-fashioned classroom with its coke stove, for example. Nevertheless, it is true and not inaccurate, the effect, such as it is, is in the detail selected for mention—the teacher's voice, putting on her coat, huddling over our milk.

Dickens in the famous passage which opens *Bleak House* describes the fog by listing the places it finds its way into: it gets in the cabman's throat, lies about in the yards, and hovers in the rigging of ships; and by doing this Dickens causes us to have mental images of each of these places. He's almost like a film director pointing his camera here and there so that we can see how bad the fog is.

T. S. Eliot describes the fog in the metaphor of a clinging dog or cat:

> *The yellow fog that rubs its back upon the window-panes,*
> *The yellow smoke that rubs its muzzle on the window-panes,*
> *Licked its tongue into the corners of the evening,*
> *Lingered upon the pools that stand in drains,*
> *Let fall upon its back the soot that falls from chimneys,*
> *Slipped by the terrace, made a sudden leap,*
> *And seeing that it was a soft October night,*
> *Curled once about the house, and fell asleep.*[1]

---

[1]From "The Love Song of J. Alfred Prufrock" in *Collected Poems* (Faber)

Eliot, of course, also uses the trick of directing our attention to the detail—the fog is on the window-panes, on the pools, it is also sooty—but intensifying it since his metaphor is organically part of the description, operating within it, so to speak, almost causing the verse to come alive literally.

I've chosen two quite different kinds of writing because I wanted to show how it is possible to get different effects. In both cases the descriptions relate to the mood or the works from which they are taken: Dickens' novel is going to be about legal fog, Eliot's poem, set in St Louis, famous for its fogs, is also recalling the past, mistily, and using the *sense* of the fog to enhance the mood.

Try writing your own piece about fog, either in prose, or in the form of a poem. It might be a memory like mine, an account of a particular place, such as a town, along a canal, a railway station. It might act as the opening of a story (see Graham Greene's *The Confidential Agent*[1]), or it might be an attempt to create an intellectual climate, a sense of obscurity for instance.

If you are really stuck, just jot down images of the fog (lights, places, animals, people, trees, etc) and then arrange them into some sort of order or pattern as a concrete poem (see p 135).

Write a short story set in some remote place in the country, or perhaps in a city, in which the main character loses his way in dense fog and arrives at a house...

WORDPLAY I

A good deal of writing is playing with words. Of course, it's a matter of seriousness to the writer that he finds the best word, the right way of saying something, to create a particular effect. Patrick White talks of milk bottles "skittering" as they are kicked over on a doorstep. In his long poem *Gaudete*[2] Ted Hughes creates the effect of a car in a couple of images that rely absolutely on the "right word":

grey Daimler
Rips the road puddles.
It rends hanging holes of
echo in the vapour-hung woods

[1]Heinemann/Penguin [2]Faber

But the process in the imagination is often a kind of play which spins off ideas, many of which are rejected, one of which is retained, modified, adapted. A useful exercise in the use of the imagination in relation to language is to take an idea or a verbal trick and to play variations on it. The following are some suggestions:

MRS WIDGETTS CALLS I was trying to write a comic novel in which at one moment the landlady, Mrs Widgetts, calls upstairs to the skulking scoundrel of a hero in a voice that would have...

shattered the nerve of a dinosaur   soured milk   coddled eggs
shattered concrete   aborted a whale   disintegrated a tank
denuded a yak   deracinated an oak   defenestrated a–
amputated a–   (Find a suitably apt or inept verb and an appropriate or inappropriate noun.)

Students might like to develop this description, or try one in which Mrs Widgetts calls in a different kind of voice – quiet, musical, sharp, soporific, etc.

OXYMORON A character in Edward Albee's *Who's Afraid of Virginia Woolf,*[1] in a parody of the pretentious kind of language one sometimes hears from rather precious critics, describes an abstract painting as having "a certain noisy relaxed quality". Whether or not such a thing is possible I think perhaps depends on the painting. However, the device can be very effective for comic and serious purposes. Think of Tennyson's "Faith unfaithful kept him falsely true", or Bacon's "Revenge is a kind of wild justice", or Joyce's "I feel a strong weakness". (See Aeolus section in *Ulysses* – p 116ff of Penguin edition– for a pyrotechnic display of figures, about a hundred altogether.) The simplest thing is to pick a noun and add an adjective with opposite or antithetical implications, eg toothless attack, aggressive complaisancy, vexatious silence/aggressive silence/truculent silence/ howling silence/turbulent quiet/thundering silence, etc. Or a variation on the foregoing: A silence so loud it would have penetrated steel, sunk a battleship, etc.

HE REMEMBERED So often one needs to say "he remembered/ thought/recalled/imagined", etc. (How many more can you think of?) But one wants to say a little more than that, and naturally the clichés present themselves, "rise in the mind", so to speak! "Memory recalled him", "recognition dawned", "his thoughts were disturbed by...". (How many more can you "recall"?) Try some variants: ideas riffled through

[1]Penguin

his mind, ideas stirred in the recesses of his thought, fragments of the past coalesced..., a thought twitched into shape, uncurled into shape/words/ideas/speech... Make up some more.

SHE SAID Another common situation is that you want to write "she said". How did she say it? Well, obviously, as with these other ideas, it will be conditioned by the play or the story, by the needs of the situation, but a useful kind of loosening up of the verbal muscles is to think of the variety of ways you can put—"she expressed a doubt", for example. In other words, you put it another way, in indirect speech or in description. The simplest way is, of course, to add an adverb: she said doubtfully/uncertainly/dubiously, etc. One can simply state what it was she said, and then describe it: She left the question in the air. Here are a few made up and developed:

> She wove endlessly inconsequential skeins of words to which the listener submitted at last, capitulated in order to escape the consequences of a reply, and was finally bound like a bobbin...
>
> She floated long streams of words about the garden, some of which might be entangled in dry twigs of dead elms, some few to drift away across the fields and end up perhaps in Wales, or distant Crete...
>
> Savoured the words in his mouth as though they were smooth rounded stones...

Or one can describe the sound of the voice—a voice like dead leaves, a voice distant as an old photograph, shaping a soundless message with her lips...

SEE next section, He said, she said.

HE SAID, SHE SAID

In writing a story or a novel one may need to use dialogue and have to make decisions how best to represent this on the page. Some writers feel that the "she asseverated roundly" or "he laughed hollowly" technique has been overworked to the point of farce, and sternly, obdurately confine themselves to "he said", "she said", or even just offer the reader dialogue and leave him to work out who said what. Sometimes we are given dialogue in the form of a play:

Paul:....
Myself:....
Andrea:....

Or we are given the reaction to the speech of another character, or the interlocutor:

Her stinging remarks left him anguished/stricken/cold/unmoved/broken/tormented with guilt...

The warmth of her voice coaxed him out of sulky annoyance...

Discuss the effectiveness of these devices and any other means of relating dialogue you have come across or may invent.

Devise some more of the "he stammered angrily" variety, and put them into a brief passage, perhaps in imitation of your favourite author or of your pet aversion:

"Dammit, Worthington!" he stammered angrily. "You go too far...". His raucous voice spluttered, misfired and stopped.

"Well, Fotheringay," rejoined the other, ingratiatingly, weedling in what his companion found an unctious and maddeningly offensive manner, "we must at all costs avoid giving annoyance to Lady...".

"To hell with Lady Angela!" bawled Fotheringay, losing all control, his voice shaking the porcelain vases on the mantelpiece, his eyes blazing, and beads of sweat forming on his forehead. "And all her blasted family!" he added, unable to formulate his thoughts into coherent sentences.

"My dear chap..." began his companion in tones that were both teasing and oleaginous, a voice that taunted and at the same time soothed, a voice that had the desired effect in causing Fotheringay to reach a deeper shade of purple so that his face was beginning to resemble an immense spherical haggis about to explode...

Carry on at will, or attempt one of your own.

Below are an assortment of words to describe disposition or remarks, which students might use, add to and/or arrange in some kind of ascending order of force from "silent", say, to "thundered":

opined	cut in	murmured	teased	rejoined
warned	mumbled	whined	barked	cooed

wheezed	sighed	burbled	gaped	ruminated
spat	confirmed	lamented	brayed	trilled
jabbed	countered	groaned	protested	scoffed
crackled	iterated	hummed	whispered	taunted
ventured	grunted	hissed	lisped	drawled

And some modifiers which might go with them:

fretfully	colourlessly	docilely	feverishly
coldly	aghast	haltingly	innocently
archly	imploringly	humiliated	unruffled
sententiously	wistfully	peevishly	portentously
unperturbed	hotly	wearily	shrilly
eloquently	probing	petulantly	piqued
defiantly	silkily	tentatively	icily

Another more demanding and possibly more interesting exercise is to try to represent someone speaking or responding in a more metaphorical vein:

she mouthed the words like some food she found loathesome
he spoke carefully savouring the words on his lips
the words broke in his throat
spitting out some gobbets of words

Students might try some of their own and then work out a piece of writing, an exchange between two characters (Fotheringay and Carruthers, Lady Fiona and Mrs Allworthy, Mary and Peter, etc) in some placid, anxious, or threatening situation.

Describe a scene in a court or the House of Commons, or at a Board Meeting or a meeting of any kind, paying particular attention to the way you represent the dialogue and the quality of voice or mood of the different speakers.

CONTRAST

There are all kinds of ways in which contrast might be used. A writer, for example, juxtaposes two characters in contrasting attitudes: for example, in *Middlemarch*[1] in the scene in which Lydgate is trying to tell Rosamund something she does not want to hear, she turns her head. Or, as in *The Alexandrian Quartet,*[2] we get contrasting views of some of the characters according to the supposed different writers of the book. But I would like to suggest a more simple and obvious kind of contrast as an exercise in writing.

This is to begin by juxtaposing opposites, or ideas that seem in some way antithetical. (The sun and moon are not exactly opposites, if you see what I mean, but some people might find them contrasting. D. H. Lawrence did, for instance.) Light—dark, low—high, open—shut, still—moving, etc. Students might jot down any pairs they like. They might confine it to obvious antonyms, but perhaps they could make it more speculative, more metaphorical: time—youth, love—time, winter—joy, etc.

Then concentrate on one idea—images of stillness, stasis, for instance; then, perhaps, images of motion. By images I simply mean verbal pictures conceived in the imagination (see p 18), though there's no reason why one shouldn't go outside and look for them. (Interestingly, even if you do that, although they are or may be *conceived* in the "real" world, they gestate in the imagination.) But I am considering that most people will be writing in a room and having to conjure up a picture from the imagination, eg a placid pool, leaves and twigs motionless, a wall; bird in flight, sea breaking over the rocks, etc. (Perhaps all things are in a state of motion—decay, regeneration, etc?)

Having done this you may find that the images themselves seem to require some kind of ordering. If so, you have probably written the first draft of a poem. (See p 165-6 for example of Yeats' first writing of his poem "Byzantium".) You might want just to go on with the ideas you have.

---

[1]George Eliot *Middlemarch* (Penguin)

[2]Lawrence Durrell *The Alexandrian Quartet* (Faber)

If not, try a different kind of contrast: say, the sea and the sky, two people, two moods, a mountain and a flower. Ted Hughes has a marvellous little poem in which he looks from the mountain to a tiny hairbell; the mountain is huge, expansive:

Being ignorant of this other, this hairbell,

That trembles, as under threats of death,
In the summer turf's heat-rise,
And in which – filling veins
Any known name of blue would bruise
Out of existence – sleeps, recovering,

The maker of the sea.[1]

Gerard Manley Hopkins devotes a whole poem to the outside contrasts in the world:

Pied Beauty

Glory be to God for dappled things –
For skies of couple-colour as a brinded cow;
For rose-moles in all stipple upon trout that swim;
Fresh-firecoal chestnut-falls; finches' wings;
Landscape plotted and pieced – fold, fallow, and plough;
And all trades, their gear and tackle and trim.

All things counter, original, spare, strange;
Whatever is fickle, freckled (who knows how?)
With swift, slow; sweet, sour; adazzle, dim:
He fathers-forth whose beauty is past change:
Praise him.

But here are the first eight lines of a sonnet, in which he is contemplating the sea and a skylark, and in doing so chooses contrasting detail ("low lull-off or all roar"):

On ear and ear two noises too old to end
Trench – right, the tide that ramps against the shore;
With a flood or a fall, low lull-off or all roar,
Frequenting there while moon shall wear and wend.

[1]From "Still Life" in *Wodwo* (Faber)

Left hand, off land, I hear the lark ascend,
[1]His rash-fresh, re-winded new-skeinèd score
In crisps of curl off wild winch whirl, and pour
And pelt music, till none's to spill nor spend.[2]

If you feel stuck, consider any contrasts there are in nature, in the natural scene, or in the town, in terms of colour, shape, texture, sound. Then consider any contrasts that emanate from personality or mood of the observer, eg in a gloomy scene the "gloom" is in the mind of the beholder, isn't it?

Find images from poems and writing you have come across, where use of contrast is marked, or interesting, or worth consideration.

---

[1]Students might like to discuss the meaning of this image before considering Hopkins's explanation in a letter which is as follows:

Rash-fresh (it is dreadful to explain these things in cold blood) means a headlong and exciting new snatch of singing, resumption by the lark of his song, which by turns he gives over and takes up again all day long...without ever losing its freshness, being a thing both new and old....The *skein* and *curl* are the lark's song which from his height gives the impression of something falling to the earth and not vertically quite but tricklingly or waveringly, something as a skein of silk ribbed by having been tightly wound on a narrow card or a notched holder or as twine or fishing tackle unwinding from a *reel* or *winch* or as pearls strung on a horsehair: the laps or folds are the notes or short measures and bars of them. The same is called a *score* in the musical sense of score and this score is 'writ upon a liquid sky trembling to welcome it', only not horizontally. The lark in wild glee *races the reel round,* paying or dealing out and down the turns of the skein or *coil* right to the earth *floor,* the ground, where it lies in a heap, as it were, or rather is all wound off on to another winch, reel, bobbin or spool in Fancy's eye, by the moment the bird touches earth and so is ready for fresh unwinding at the next flight....*Crisp* means almost *crisped,* namely with notes.

Letter, May 1882 to Bridges, quoted by Bridges in his edition of *Poems of Gerard Manley Hopkins* (OUP)

[2]"The Sea and the Skylark"

VIEWPOINT

('I'm twenty-two. It's nearly the end of October. Life is thoroughly pleasant, although unfortunately there are a great number of fools about. One must apply oneself to something or other – God knows what. Everything is really very jolly – except getting up in the morning and wearing a tail coat.')

'I say, Bonamy, what about Beethoven?'

('Bonamy is an amazing fellow. He knows practically everything – not more about English literature than I do – but then he's read all those Frenchmen.')

'I rather suspect you're talking rot, Bonamy. In spite of what you say, poor old Tennyson...'

('The truth is one ought to have been taught French. Now, I suppose, old Barfoot is talking to my mother. That's an odd affair to be sure. But I can't see Bonamy down there. Damn London!') for the market carts were lumbering down the street.

'What about a walk on Saturday?'

('What's happening on Saturday?')

Then, taking out his pocket-book, he assured himself that the night of the Durrants' party came next week.

But though all this may very well be true – so Jacob thought and spoke – so he crossed his legs – filled his pipe – sipped his whisky, and once looked at his pocket-book, rumpling his hair as he did so, there remains over something which can never be conveyed to a second person save by Jacob himself. Moreover, part of this is not Jacob but Richard Bonamy – the room; the market carts; the hour; the very moment of history. Then consider the effect of sex – how between man and woman it hangs wavy, tremulous, so that here's a valley, there's a peak, when in truth, perhaps, all's as flat as my hand. Even the exact words get the wrong accent on them. But something is always impelling one to hum vibrating, like the hawk moth, at the mouth of the cavern of mystery, endowing Jacob Flanders with all sorts of qualities he had not at all – for though, certainly he sat talking to Bonamy, half of what he said was too dull to repeat; much unintelligible (about unknown people and Parliament); what remains is mostly a matter of guess work. Yet over him we hang vibrating.

In this extract from her novel *Jacob's Room*[1] Virginia Woolf is representing the thoughts of her character, Jacob, (the bits in parenthesis) and what is going on in the world outside him, and she is also, in the final paragraph, reflecting as narrator on the problems that face the novelist, on how best to present her material. We all, like Jacob, have an interior life that is personal to us and which only we can know, though we may be able to offer bits of it to others; we also have a public life in which other people see us and form opinions; we exist in the mind of others as fragments, memories, impressions—perhaps, at any single moment, as we stand in a room, say, looking out of the window at the street below, we have our private existence, and at the same time people we know exist elsewhere and we are lodged somewhere in their memory banks, or possibly, even, impressions of us come to the surface of their minds. The problem the writer faces is how best to represent what he takes to be reality. He can be godlike seeing into the lives of all. He can be locked inside one head in a first-person narrative. He can move between the two.

The choice of viewpoint presents a challenge and a limitation to the writer. Many writers cut their losses and work within a convention, only allowing into the novel what the convention allows. If it's a first-person narrative, say, then the main character can only know what people tell him, or what he can guess about them, as in *David Copperfield,* for instance. Or writers may experiment, as Dickens did in *Bleak House,* where he alternates chapters written from the omnipotent viewpoint and chapters written as the diary or first-person narrative of Esther Summerson. Joyce in *Ulysses* seized the dilemma and broke it apart, employing a whole range of techniques: interior monologue, third-person narrative with single-person viewpoint, the omnipotent viewpoint, multi-viewpoint, etc. In fact, anyone interested in the techniques of writing can't afford not to look at *Ulysses* and will find it a veritable manual of devices.

In *Jacob's Room* Mrs Woolf was trying, a little more modestly perhaps, to take up the challenges the problem presents and show her character from different viewpoints, at the same time attempting to give a flavour of the essentially "fragmentary" nature of our experience. In an essay on modern fiction which she wrote in 1919[2]

---

[1]Hogarth Press/Penguin

[2]"The Modern Novel" in *The Common Reader* (Hogarth Press)

Virginia Woolf argues that life is very different from the life the novelist is constrained by convention to present:

> Must novels be like this?
> Look within and life, it seems, is very far from being 'like this'. Examine for a moment an ordinary mind on an ordinary day. The mind receives a myriad of impressions—trivial, fantastic, evanescent, or engraved with the sharpness of steel. From all sides they come, an incessant shower of innumerable atoms; and as they fall, as they shape themselves into the life of Monday or Tuesday, the accent falls differently from of old; the moment of importance came not here but there; so that if a writer were a free man and not a slave, if he could write what he chose, not what he must, if he could base his work upon his own feeling and not upon convention, there would be no plot, no comedy, no tragedy, no love interest or catastrophe in the accepted sense, and perhaps not a single button sown on as the Bond Street tailors would have it. Life is not a series of gig-lamps symmetrically arranged; life is a luminous halo, a semi-transparent envelope surrounding us from the beginning of consciousness to the end. Is it not the task of the novelist to convey this varying, this unknown and uncircumscibed spirit, whatever aberration or complexity it may display, with as little mixture of the alien and external as possible?

If you are interested in experimenting with viewpoint, you might begin with a simple situation—a country house, say, to which you have been invited, with perhaps a dozen people. It might be a party, or a course you are on. During the weekend something disappears, something trivial or valuable or of sentimental value to one of the guests. Or if you find the scene too exalted, set it in a cottage, or on a housing estate. This will probably affect the characters and their reactions; there might be sociological and emotional implications you might want to exploit. However, the object disappears. Now write about it from the viewpoint of the different characters, perhaps ending with a multi-viewpoint approach.

Another idea is to take two characters, and examine from the viewpoint of each in turn an event or alternatively a piece of news: "Have you heard that George has married Martha?" Suppose each of them has different feelings or knowledge about George and about Martha:

"I've never liked George. He was too pushing."

"What? George? He was never pushing. Quiet chap, very

reserved...' etc.

In a fascinating story called "Flowers for Algernon"[1] Daniel Keyes utilizes the restrictions of first-person narrative brilliantly. Charlie Gordon keeps a diary. He is mentally subnormal, has an operation and treatment which gradually increases his intelligence to the point where he becomes a genius, only to find his intellect deteriorating as the effects of the operation wear off. Charlie charts his intellectual and emotional development, his love for the nurse Miss Kinnian, etc. And, of course, the fact that we are contained inside Charlie's head adds enormously to the power of the story. Students might like to read and discuss the story and consider stories of their own where they might attempt this technique.

Elsewhere (p 62ff) I suggest that students keep a commonplace book or notebook in which, among other things, they might enter brief stories or items from the news. One of these might be used to try out a story from different points of view. For example:

> He said that the older boy, Rob, had suggested they go for a walk around Woolworths, but that he became afraid when Rob began to take things from the counters.

Assuming this to be the truth (though there might be other explanations), it would be interesting to tell the story from the frightened boy's viewpoint, either in the first person (perhaps in a monologue, or dialogue with policeman, Headmaster, etc), or in the third person with a first-person perspective, or from a detached third-person viewpoint which just states what happens and with no interpretation.

Another example:

> The mini-submarine with four men on board, trapped off Key West, Florida, has surfaced. Condition of crew unknown.[2]

All sorts of interesting possibilities here. For a student interested in hardware there is the opportunity for use of technical information: references to pressure, oxygen supply, depth, fuel, conservation of energy, etc; so the log of the events would be quite intriguing (one viewpoint). Then the tensions in the relationships between the men would be worth exploring. What sort of personalities? What about their backgrounds and lives? Well, they might spend time telling each other about their lives, their past, etc. Someone's nerve might

---

[1]See *Points of View* Ed. James Moffatt and Kenneth R. McElheny (Mentor Books)

[2]*Guardian* newspapers

break. The incident might be presented in the form of a letter, diary, dialogue, etc.

For those who find the technical aspects of the drama too daunting, imagine the same situation in a pothole, cave or tunnel, with two or more people trapped for a period, say a day or a few hours. Incidentally the first radio play, *Danger,*[1] was about some people trapped in a mine. It was thought that the idea of darkness would help the listener to imagine the situation since the characters would emerge as "voices in the dark". What about that as a title?

Finally, as a kind of extension of an idea mentioned earlier (the boy in Woolworths), suppose the Headmaster of his school has received a telephone call about the boy from the manager of the store. Start from the point when the boy knocks on the Headmaster's door. Then decide whether you should best put it into third-person narrative (eg when the boy is unjustly accused, or internally pondering whether to involve, to "tell on" his companion). Another way to approach it is to imagine it as a radio play in which inner thoughts can be presented by change in the tone of the voice, nearness to microphone, etc.

Some students may be interested in the earlier quotations from Virginia Woolf and want to attempt some work arising out of that. I suggest you begin with a character in a room, looking at the wall, a book, an object, and give some indication of the person's thoughts; then move to a different perspective—say that of someone passing by the window and noticing your first character. Or have your character walking along a street and try to present him from the viewpoint of the people he passes or encounters; you might even take into consideration what people are thinking of him at that moment.

OTHER EXAMPLES

See stories in *Points of View* Ed. James Moffatt and Kenneth R. McElheny (Mentor Books), especially:
"But the One on the Right" Dorothy Parker
"The Use of Force" William Carlos Williams
"The Prison" Bernard Malamud
"The Boarding House" James Joyce

---

[1]Richard Hughes (BBC)

Opening of *There is a Happy Land* Keith Waterhouse (Penguin)
Opening of *The Go-Between* L. P. Hartley (Faber)
Extract from *The Eye of the Storm* Patrick White (Penguin)
(See p 93 this book)
Opening of *Trawl* B. S. Johnson (Panther) (See p 157 this book)

USE OF THE IMAGINATION II OBSERVATION

In the first attempt to draw attention to the way it is possible to exercise our imagination with the simple raw material of common experience (p 23) I used the theme of getting up in the morning and the ordinary everyday impressions we might have. Here I'd like to consider the world around us and ways in which it may provide the impetus to write. Particularly, I'd like to draw on the notebooks of one writer, Gerard Manley Hopkins, who seems to have made it an almost daily task to note down his experiences. It seems to me likely that, just as an athlete may need to exercise every day to keep fit, so anyone who wants to use language in a vital fashion may find it helpful to write something every day.[1]

Students should enter any kind of impressions in their commonplace books, however trivial or "commonplace" they might seem (eating porridge, the rain falling from leaves, watching a man wheel a wheelbarrow, the movements of a cat on a wall, etc). Try to get down as much detail as possible. Having done that, it is a good idea to examine the words you have chosen. Are they the first words that came to hand? Are there better ones? Do the words themselves have their own form? (Norman MacCaig draws attention to this problem

[1]Mrs Thomas described young Dylan as a small boy happy with a bit of paper and pencil describing the boiler on washday. William Golding talks of his fascination as a child with the sound of words.

in his poem "An Ordinary Day", q.v. p 171.) The words themselves alter the observation, alter our impressions; they transform what are presumably chemical or electrical responses in the brain and the nervous system into a set of semantic relationships and perhaps auditory relationships (if we say them out loud) of their own. Here is an example of what I mean from the Notebooks of Gerard Manley Hopkins:

> Drops of rain hanging on rails etc. seen with only the lower rim lighted like nails (of fingers). Screws of brooks and twines. Soft chalky look with more shadowy middles of the globes of cloud on a night with a moon faint or concealed. Mealy clouds with a not brilliant moon. Blunt buds of the ash. Pencil buds of the beech. Lobes of the trees. Cups of the eyes, Gathering back the lightly hinged eyelids. Bows of the eyelids. Pencil of eyelashes. Juices of the eyeball. Eyelids like leaves, petals, caps, tufted hats, handkerchiefs, sleeves, gloves. Also of the bones sleeved in flesh. Juices of the sunrise. Joins and veins the same. Vermillion look of the hand held against a candle with the darker parts as the middles of the fingers and especially the knuckles covered with ash.[1]

Apart from the variety and richness of the actual impressions noted by Hopkins, it is interesting to consider the way his verbal faculties are operating: the "rails" in the first line, perhaps by unconscious rhyme, throws up the "nails" in the second. "Nails (of fingers)," he points out, but there are other kinds of nails, and it is no doubt this other kind that he has connected with them in his unconscious, so bringing "screws" to the surface of his imagination. Then notice the incipient metaphor beginning to take shape (if he wished to use it) in the exploration of the "Blunt buds"—"Lobes"—"Cups of the eyes" sequence of images. I think here we can see the poetic imagination at work in its early initiating process: the writer notices something in nature; in the attempt to record his impressions, the means of recording—*words*—begins to establish an order of its own, to connect in sound and meaning. Obviously, had he wished to do so, Hopkins could have worked at this material and fashioned it into a poem. Here is an extract from one of his later poems "That Nature is a Heraclitean Fire", in which one can see the processes noted above more tightly organized:

---

[1] 1866

Cloud-puffball, torn-tufts, tossed pillows flaunt forth,
then chevy on an air –
built thoroughfare: heaven-roysterers, in gay-gangs
they throng; they glitter in marches.
Down roughcast, down dazzling whitewash, wherever an
elm arches,
Shivelights and shadowtackle in long lashes lace, lance,
and pair.

Elsewhere in the notebooks we see the poet concentrating specifically on words and their connections and relations:

> *Grind, gride, gird, grit, groat, grate, greet, κρουειν, crush, crash, κροτειν,* etc.
>
> Original meaning to *strike, rub,* particularly *together.* That which is produced by such means is the *grit,* the *groats* or crumbs, like *fragmentum* from *frangere, bit* from *bite. Crumb, crumble,* perhaps akin. To *greet,* to strike hands together (?). *Greet,* grief, wearing, *tribulation. Grief* possibly connected. *Gruff,* with a sound as of two things rubbing together. I believe these words to be onomatopoetic. *Gr* common to them all representing a particular sound. In fact I think the onomatopoetic theory has not had a fair chance. Cf. *crack, creak, croak, crake, graculus, crackle.* These must be onomatopoetic.[1]

Students might find it profitable to engage in similar speculations of their own in relation to words they find themselves interested in.

Before we leave this section on observation I think it might be relevant to choose another extract from a notebook, this time from that of a painter, perhaps noticing in what ways, if any, the painter's eye differs from that of the poet. Leonardo da Vinci wrote in his Notebooks:

> Observe the motion of the surface of the water, how it resembles that of hair, which has two movements – one depends on the weight of the hair, the other on the direction of the curls; thus the water forms whirling eddies, one part following the impetus of the chief current, and the other following the incidental motion and return flow.[2]

Leonardo's observation of the water leads him to a kind of visual metaphor of human hair, and one can see in his sketches attempts to

[1] 1863
[2] From *Selections from the Notebooks of Leonardo da Vinci* Ed. Irma A. Richter (OUP)

draw hair as water, and vice versa.

So students might like to consider these ideas in relation to their own observations, to the variety of detail of the actual impressions, the words they choose to represent these, and the presence of emerging metaphor in their notes. Having made these rough notes, they should look to see if there is any kind of form or pattern in their arrangement—it may be that the form is there latent and needs only a little push to get it into shape.

Observation

Now and then concentrating
on the very small,

focusing my attention
on a very small area

like this crack in sandstone
perpetually wet with seepage,

getting so close
to moss, liverwort and fern

it becomes a forest
with wild beasts in it,

birds in the branches
and crickets piping,

cicadas shrilling.
Someone seeing me

staring so fixedly
at nothing

might be excused
for thinking me vague, abstracted,

lost in introspection.
No! I am awake, absorbed,

just looking in a different direction.

W. Hart-Smith[1]

SEE also "The Thing Made Real" by Ron Loewinsohn on p 177

[1]In *The Unceasing Ground* (Angus & Robertson (UK) Ltd)

SHE LOOKED UP

A character often looks at, up, down, across, etc, in a story: that is, she *responds* to some remark, to a letter, to an object, without necessarily saying anything. The look indicates the feelings of the character, or perhaps the look is obscure, baffling, disconcerting, or perhaps the character avoids looking at all. Lawrence Durrell in describing a character in his novel *Justine*[1] says the man avoids a direct glance:

> In not looking at you he is sparing you from a regard so pitiless that it would disconcert you for an evening.

Students might find it worthwhile, as a piece of general observation of people, to find an appropriate way of describing their looks. Is the look open or obscure? Direct, challenging, aggressive, or warm, friendly? Or is it alluring, inviting? These are just general responses and there are innumerable intermediate aspects of the response, from the uninvolved or neutral to the very strongly felt. Apart from "looks", "stares", and "gazes", there are ways of describing the eyes which might give a clue to the feelings, from the obvious "bright" or "dull" to the intermediate or slightly strange or mystic "glaucus", or the metaphoric "flickered like a bird's eye", "eyes impenetrable as cats'", where the use of metaphor takes over and enforces a new and maybe less tangible quality in the description. Sometimes in a piece of writing a single word is effective: "Her eyes were cool/smiling/pitiless." Sometimes it is more telling to build up a description through several lines or sentences. You may wish to leave your reader with a burning, traumatic, frenzied, etc, sensation of the character's eyes. (Suppose he's a hypnotist, madman, ghost, or someone haunted...)

Below are some assorted descriptions of looks. Students might like to add to them, ignore them and make up their own, arrange them in various orders (from uninvolved to assaulting, from gentle to ferocious, etc), or use them or some of them as the basis for a character description, or for a scene. For example, you might try a

---

[1]Faber

merciless parody of the writer you think most guilty of over-writing in this way:

> Lady Cynthia flashed him a look of recognition. It was also the gaze of the frightened child, a look so imploring that his heart melted.
>
> "My darling," he murmured, casting a look of hope mixed with the anguish of despair, a look at once dark and burning, humble and challenging. She felt his gaze burn into her very being. She returned the look of a hunted doe, but in that look there was something of the eagle soaring, the bird of paradise exotic in its opulent, luxurious plumage, as well as the gentle dove.
>
> He enfolded her in his dark, hairy arms, the shoulders of which were torn and bleeding. Her eyes melted with pity at the sight.
>
> "Jason!" The word caressed her lips. She looked back into his eyes, burning with passion, inconsolable with humility, tortured with longing.
>
> "Cynthia!" His voice was hoarse with a wild, terrible energy seething in those flaming eyes...

Carry on at leisure.

Or you might find this too capricious and want something more serious or demanding. Take a simple scene in which some information is being imparted, something very moving or sad perphaps:

1) American Civil War—son returning to farm tells mother that brother is dead.
2) A mute person—child or adult—terrified, pleased, happy, wanting to communicate. Describe looks.
3) A seaman picked up out of the sea in north Atlantic having been in water several days.
4) Meeting a man who has stayed the night alone in a haunted house. You are a reporter.
5) Examine people's expressions in photographs—your own or those brought along by tutor—or choose some from newspapers and magazines and attempt to put the expression or look into words.
6) Write a scene from a novel in which four characters meet. They could either be unknown to each other, or meet after a long absence, after some important event or adventure.

WORDS AND EXPRESSIONS

looked up gazed glanced darted a look/glance
peered stared glared scrutinized enquiring look

curious stare squinted squinnyed eyes narrowed eyes wide open eyes flashed blazed limpid expression burning dull dead incandescent furtive look self-satisfied look look of abject terror despairing inscrutible searing freezing harrowing penetrating disdainful look of hauteur envious glance purient stare look of menace searching exhaustive stare

DIALOGUE

Harold Pinter: What is so different about the stage is that you're just *there,* stuck—there are your characters stuck on the stage, you've got to live with them and deal with them. I'm not a very inventive writer in the sense of using technical devices other playwrights do—look at Brecht! I can't use the stage the way he does. I just haven't got that kind of imagination, so I find myself stuck with these characters who are either sitting or standing, and they've got to walk out of a door, or come in through a door, and that's about all they can do.
Interviewer: And talk.
Pinter: Or keep silent.[1]

Obviously all sorts of considerations are going to affect the nature of the dialogue in a piece of writing. If the director insists on using the elephant he has hired for a week, one of the characters is going to have to say something about it. Or *avoid* saying something about it, which might leave a lacuna in the dialogue, which is itself a kind of comment. But Harold Pinter's argument is surely valid. You have these characters and they are talking or keeping silent. What they say may depend on their personality, their situation, the author's need to further the action, convey information. Think of the radio plays that have this kind of exchange:

A: It's a sunny day, isn't it?
B: I always think the park looks lovely in the spring.
C: The riding habit suits you, although the 375 biretta you're carrying in your shoulder holster alters the line of the jacket...

[1]Interview with Harold Pinter from *The Playwrights Speak* Ed. Walter Wagner (Longman)

But the credibility of the characters' dialogue and the reader's or viewer's involvement with it (certainly on stage) depends not only on the nature of what is being said in the context, but also on those tricks of speech, verbal gestures, idiosyncracies, etc, which convey the sense of personality. Pinter is particularly adept in exploiting these matters, indeed even using them almost as plot. In the short dramatic sequence for two characters, "Last to Go",[1] this is vividly illustrated:

A Coffee stall. A barman and an old newspaper seller.

Silence
Man: You was a bit busy earlier.
Barman: Ah.
M: Round about ten.
B: Ten, was it?
M: About then.
(Pause.)
I passed by here about then.
B: Oh yes?
M: I noticed you were doing a bit of trade.
(Pause.)
B: Yes, trade was very brisk about ten.
M: Yes, I noticed.
(Pause.)
I sold my last one about then. Yes. About nine forty-five.
B: Sold your last then, did you?
M: Yes, my last *Evening News* it was. Went about twenty to ten.
(Pause.)
B: *Evening News,* was it?
M: Yes.
(Pause.)
Sometimes it's the *Star* is the last to go.
B: Ah.
M: Or the...Whatsisname.
B: *Standard*
M: Yes.
(Pause.)
All I had left tonight was the *Evening News.*
(Pause.)

[1]In *A Slight Ache and Other Plays* (Methuen)

B: Then that went, did it?
M: Yes.
(Pause.)
Like a shot.
(Pause.)
B: You didn't have any left, eh?
M: No. Not after I sold that one.
(Pause.)
B: It was after that you must have come by here then, was it?
M: Yes, I come by here after that, see, after I packed up.
B: You didn't stop here though, did you?
M: When?
B: I mean, you didn't stop here and have a cup of tea then, did you?
M: What, about ten?
B: Yes.
M: No, I went up to Victoria.
B: No, I thought I didn't see you.
M: I had to up to Victoria.
(Pause.)
B: Yes, trade was very brisk here about ten.
(Pause.)
M: I went to see if I could get hold of George.
B: Who?
M: George.
(Pause.)
B: George who?
M: George...Whatsisname.
B: Oh.
(Pause.)
Did you get hold of him?
M: No. No, I couldn't get hold of him. I couldn't locate him.
B: He's not about much now, is he?
(Pause.)
M: When did you last see him then?
B: Oh, I haven't seen him for years.
M: No, nor me.
(Pause.)
B: Used to suffer very bad from arthritis.
M: Arthritis?
B: Yes.

M: He never suffered from arthritis.
B: Suffered very bad.
(Pause.)
M: Not when I knew him.
(Pause.)
B: I think he must have left the area.
(Pause.)
M: Yes, it was the *Evening News* was the last to go tonight.
B: Not always the last though, is it, though?
M: No, oh no. I mean sometimes it's the *News*. Other times it's one of the others. No way of telling beforehand. Until you've got your last one left, of course. Then you can tell which one it's going to be.
B: Yes.
(Pause.)
M: Oh yes.
(Pause.)
I think he must have left the area.

Note here how the dialogue moves in little sequences: exchange about trade, then about selling the last one, then about George, George's arthritis, then a sort of final recapitulation of all the ingredients of the dialogue.

At this point students might do a piece of writing using two or three characters engaged in desultory exchanges, or in conversation on some specific topic (eg the way a goal was scored, the price of fish, etc). Notice how Pinter's ear is attuned to characteristic modes of speech:

M: He never suffered from arthritis.
B: Suffered very bad.
(Pause.)

Also note the self-conscious use of the unusual word: "I couldn't get hold of him. I couldn't *locate* him"; and the significant pauses, suggesting inability to follow what has been said, or perhaps representing self-preoccupation. Notice, too, that as so often happens, one character is dominant, one subordinate, perhaps only briefly, then one retreats, or ignores what has been said. In *The Caretaker* and *The Birthday Party* Pinter relies a good deal, for the sense of menace in the plays, on this dominant—subordinate technique.

Students might separate these processes out, in writing first a piece which simply conveys the nature of the dialogue situation, then another (or perhaps rewrite the first) introducing the dominant role motif (eg "Of course he's always been a better player! When did you see Charleton score four in a row? Eh? Come on. You haven't, have you? Admit it?" etc).

Sometimes, particularly with Shakespeare, the intention is to show something of the background, life style, perhaps even the faults latent in the character about whom we might have diverse opinions. Othello, for example, tantalizes us, just as he had engaged the affections of Desdemona, with the exotic story of his life, a rich life full of action and adventure, and it is possible that his creator is hinting that he might be gulling himself a little with the glamour of it.[1] Certainly it is a forceful and seductive picture of the traveller embroidering his experiences and Olivier brought this out in his famous and, in certain respects, controversial National Theatre production.

Her father lov'd me; oft invited me,
Still question'd me the story of my life,
From year to year; the battles, sieges, fortunes,
That I have pass'd:
I ran it through, even from my boyish days,
To the very moment that he bade me tell it.
Wherein I spoke of most disastrous chances,
Of moving accidents by flood and field;
Of hair-breadth 'scapes i' the imminent deadly breach;
Of being taken by the insolent foe;
And sold to slavery, of my redemption thence,
And with it all my travel's history;
Wherein of antres vast, and deserts idle,
Rough quarries, rocks, and hills, whose heads touch heaven,
It was my hint to speak, such was the process:—
And of the Cannibals, that each other eat;
The Anthropophagi, and men whose heads
Do grow beneath their shoulders: this to hear
Would Desdemona seriously incline;
But still the house-affairs would draw her thence,
And ever as she could with haste despatch,

---

[1]Of course it should be said that, since many of his audience would have found Othello's marvels credible, Shakespeare may not have intended to show his hero as exaggerating. Still, it seems the possibility is there.

She'ld come again, and with a greedy ear
Devour up my discourse; which I observing,
Took once a pliant hour, and found good means
To draw from her a prayer of earnest heart,
That I would all my pilgrimage dilate...[1]

Students might attempt another bit of writing here. Some historical figure, perhaps, whom they have some knowledge of or interest in, might be represented at a crucial moment in his career: a fifteenth-century Count imprisoned in a fortress (Sforza, for example) (see p 117), or Luther before a congregation, Galileo before the Inquisition, Anne Boleyn before her accusers, etc.

This is perhaps a good place to introduce the theme of trial or interrogation (see also p 115ff). Many writers have extracted a good deal of drama from the court-room or the interrogation cell: Shakespeare in *The Merchant of Venice,* Ibsen in *Enemy of the People,* Miller in *The Crucible,* Shaw in *Saint Joan,* Osborne in *Luther* and *Subject of Scandal and Concern;* also the novels: Kafka's *The Trial,* David Karp's *One,* Koestler's *Darkness before Noon,* Orwell's *Nineteen Eighty-Four,* etc. Perhaps students would like to attempt another piece using some of the above ideas—verbal tricks, idiosyncracies of speech, hesitation, silence, etc— together with some background material to reinforce the character, as Shakespeare does in the Othello episode. It might be made more interesting by introducing some element of challenge, such as in a court room or interrogation scene: imagine, for instance, Mark Antony before the Senate in Rome trying to defend himself against accusations of betrayal, ineptitude, etc; Richard Nixon defending his part in Watergate; an American unit commander charged with killing civilians in Vietnam; Dickens repudiating charges of distortion in the writing of *Oliver Twist,* etc.

Of course, the situation itself is important. The German playwright Ashkenazy has a play which begins with a telephone call from a distressed girl in a telephone kiosk, asking for the Samaritans. A man replies that she obviously has the wrong number. The play goes on to explore the relationship.

[1]Act I sc. iii l. 127—70 (Arden Shakespeare)

Students might find this an appealing exercise to try out, possibly in the form of a tape. If you feel stuck, begin:

Phone rings.
Caller: Look, you don't know me and I don't know you, but this is important. Don't hang up. I've dialled the first number that came into my head. Look, this may be my last opportunity to tell...

(A man, woman, child in distress? Caused by what? Fear, obsessed with guilt, an imaginary obsession, some macabre, weird series of events, the last man on earth?)

The following are some suggestions for dialogue or monologue. Obviously you can employ the techniques or ideas mentioned above; you can use more than two people; you can use a narrator if you want to; you can complicate it by including (especially if you are trying the form of a radio play) what goes on in the characters' minds or imaginations, as in Dylan Thomas's *Under Milk Wood* or Ted Hughes' "The Wound" (Look up both. The Hughes play is to be found in *Wodwo*[1]).

You can, if you like the challenge, develop your choice into a phantasmagoria of some kind, in which people from history, fiction, myth, coalesce or appear as individuals, as in Eliot's "The Waste Land" or the Circe episode in Joyce's *Ulysses.*

OTHER SUGGESTIONS

1) You (an imaginary character or yourself) can go back to a place you knew when you were young, and interview people, eg a teacher, man you worked with, neighbour, etc. See Dylan Thomas's "Return Journey".
2) Husband and wife at breakfast. (Who? Where? When? Are they agreeable, bored, antagonistic, reflective, cunning, subtle, intelligent, dumb, etc?) If you are stuck or uncertain, make the husband a failed comedian/violinist/clown/ex-king, and the wife, a yachtswoman/bus conductress/opera-singer/typist/GP/hairdresser/cleaner, etc.
3) Two men, women, old or young, children, tramps, 'cellists, roof-felters, etc, sit on park bench, in art gallery, café, etc.
4) The prisoner. (See above and p 115ff). Choose place, period, time, character, eg French Revolution, Spanish Inquisition, Greece under Colonels, Great Britain in Civil war, or at the present.

[1]Faber

5) Conversation on a train. (An old-fashioned train with no corridor?)
6) Interview by Headmaster of boy accused of some misdemeanour or crime (stealing, smoking, reading pornography, being abusive, writing poetry in Geography lesson, etc). Is he guilty? Leave it in doubt?
7) Children in playground, recreation ground, somewhere where they shouldn't be.
8) Trapped in cave, pothole, on mountain side, tent in blizzard, in open boat.
9) Read Robert Graves's "Welsh Incident" (see p 168). Try a piece on a similar theme.
10) Illogical conversation half heard/overheard on a bus.
11) *A la recherche du temps perdu.* Memories of past. An old man or woman remembers. Use voices, sounds, music, etc.
12) Imaginary conversation.

OTHER MATERIAL

Harold Pinter "Landscape" in *Landscape and Silence* (Methuen)
Tony Hancock "The Radio Ham" on *The Best of Tony Hancock* (Halmark HMA 228)
Robert Browning "Fra Lippo Lippi", "Andrea Del Sarto"
Samuel Beckett *Krapp's Last Tape* (Faber)

PLACES I REMEMBER

...all my lifetime, though some have changed...

Places are important to us in locating a memory, a person, a sense of a moment past. Consider the effect of a Dutch interior painting. There's one in the National Gallery of a woman sitting, her arm resting on her elbow, asleep, and surrounded by dishes waiting to be washed. She's obviously worn out, oblivious. Above her stands another woman looking at us, the viewers, and holding out her hand as if to say, "Well, and what do you think of that?" She has a smile on her face, indicating a little indulgence of the sleeping woman. In the background people are sitting, talking and eating. On the cupboard the cat is just about to steal the duck. The painting by

Nicholas Maes is called *The Idle Servant*. In another painting, by Vermeer, called *A View of Delft,* two women with shopping baskets walk towards some other people by a boat; over on the other side of the canal are buildings and a bridge; some cloud has just collected and it looks as if there's going to be a shower—a particular place at a particular time, making the kind of impression in the mind that reality might make, leaving an image there, to be recalled much later and with great vividness.

Think of places you know, or have an image of. It might be anywhere. For me, just thinking aloud, there is an image of a corner shop I used to pass on the way to school. I don't remember the shop so much as the square of blue, almost shiny black, pavement in front of it, and a low wall also of blue industrial brick, capped with round coping stones of the same material, polished because we used to sit on it and straddle our legs, kicking our heels against it. Your image might be a garden, a pool, an alleyway, a playground, a market, a bit of waste ground, a coppice—anywhere. Concentrate on one image for a moment. Jot down some words to help fix it. It may be that if you are good at visualizing, there will be enough in that single image for you to explore, as a child might trace with his mind's eye the elaborate contours of his desk. It may be that there is not just one image but a plethora—a cat arching its back on a wall, behind that a chestnut tree covered with brown falling leaves, part of a water-spout, etc, etc. Write the images down. Arrange them in a way you find effective. This might be as a series of discrete images, a loose kind of poem. It might be as a piece of descriptive prose which you might like to arrange so that the readers' eyes move from one thing to the next in some kind of sequence. (See the extract from the opening of Iris Murdoch's *The Sandcastle* p 38 this book).

Students might make a list of places for which they have particular feelings of affection, fear, etc. Select one and describe it in a page or so.

But places also have their own individual quality—a railway station, a seaside cafe, a recreation ground. In the opening of *The Confidential Agent,* Graham Greene is describing a boat arriving at Dover from across the Channel. In these paragraphs we get the sense of the motion of the ship, the shrieking of the gulls, the fog, the rush of passengers. If you've ever come into harbour on a boat at night, you recognize it immediately.

Choose a place, such as one of the above mentioned, or a mountain in Wales, or the Lakes, a park, amusement arcade, cinema, disco, library, gasworks, etc, and try to imagine it in as much detail as you can—the sounds, the smells of the place, anything, in fact, which is characteristic, which makes it unique. Then write down your ideas. When you've done that, look through it. Can you, by adding an image (such as Greene's image of the gulls like "hysterical women" in the shrouds), or a particular word, maybe a technical word, "fix" the description? For example, the word "jetty" is a specific word which might help to locate a place (what are the words to describe the structure that supports it?); or you might refer to the engines of a boat ("pistons pounding in reverse"); or suppose it's a forest and you want to describe the trees—what kinds? A country house might have terraces, balustrades, parapets. The seashore might have shingle, flotsam, tar, limpets, marl, silt, groyne, buoy, hulk, spar, etc, etc.

OTHER EXAMPLES
Len Deighton *Horse Under Water* Penguin edition p 16ff (Naval Dockyard)
Anthony Burgess *Honey for the Bears* Chap. 7 (Astoria Hotel)
Charles Dickens *Bleak House* Opening (City River, etc)
Patrick White *The Tree of Man* Opening (Bush)

DETAIL I

> She stubbed out her cigarette now and, deep in thought, rose to walk up and down the room, her hands hugged in her armpits. As always when she was thinking deeply, she moved in a strange almost awkward way—a prowling walk which reminded him of some predatory animal...[1]

For me the detail of Justine, "her hands hugged in her armpits", realizes this scene very clearly. In *A Severed Head* Iris Murdoch's first-person narrator is waiting in a hotel lounge, his arm resting on the bar, behind a newspaper, trying to catch someone leaving the country; the character is apprehensive and emotional, his arm begins to ache as he has been sitting awkwardly. That little detail of the

[1]Lawrence Durrell *Mountolive* (Faber)

aching arm puts the seal on the rest of the description. It is often some physical detail of this kind which gives a moment or a character verisimilitude. The writer has to imagine or visualize in his head such detail which may not be immediately relevant, but it has to come in the first place from observation, from noticing that men sometimes hitch the waistband of their trousers, lift their spectacles on thumb and forefinger to rub the red weals on the bridge of their noses, remove a leaf of cigarette paper from a lower lip etc.

There are dozens of such gestures, behaviour patterns, movements, which we tend to perform and which *place* us—apart from personal idiosyncracies like scratching the side of a forehead with an index finger when there is no need to scratch it, a nervous tic in fact. Students interested in writing might make it a practice to notice such features of behaviour. Here are a few around which you might try to build some scene, or which you might like to discuss or use as a starter in compiling a mental repertory of such human detail:

standing, backs of hands on hips, elbows forward
standing, hands in pockets, the weight on one leg
arms folded under her breasts supporting them
put his outspread hands to his back, stretching as though afflicted with backache
sitting one thigh crossing the other, a foot hooked behind a calf
massaging eyes with palms of his hands as though tired
removing a long hair from her sleeve
pursing lips, sucking in lips, moistening lips
tapping teeth with a pencil
reflectively scratching the back of his hand
rubbing pipe on his nose so that both began to gleam
twisting a shank of lank or loose hair behind an ear in a delicate intimate gesture
coyly sucking the end of a forefinger
smoothing out her skirt over her thighs
stuffing the seams of gloves into the fingers in a nervous gesture
picking at hole in the end of one of the fingers of his gloves
leaning forward to glide a hand along her shin, massaging the ankle
blowing his nose with great violence into a huge handkerchief
making a pyramid with extended fingers
pushing her shoes under the table, she rubbed one stockinged foot against another

looped a finger inside a shoulder strap to ease her bosom
rotating her gold wedding ring with nervous anxiety

The list is endless, apparently. Clearly, these are features of behaviour I've noticed and they would impinge on my mind in a book. It doesn't follow that everyone would regard them in the same way, or find them meaningful in placing a character, but I hope there is enough variety here to give some idea of the kind of thing I mean, and that students will find it interesting to notice such features. Notice them in books as well as in life and try to describe a scene, say in a café or pub, in terms of the behaviour of the people there. And, knocking out the dottle of my pipe into the glass ashtray, I leave you with these thoughts...

GIRL ON A BICYCLE

Every day of our lives we have innumerable little experiences, little encounters with reality, so to speak, which in turn may lead to fantasy. A boy sees a girl riding a bicycle, she makes an impression on him—her raincoat, her hair, her legs, the way the bicycle wobbles, the expression on her face, and so on: these things register in his mind. Maybe he fantasizes more extravagantly about her, sexually, or emotionally, or idealistically. Maybe he's just curious. Who is she? Where does she come from? What is she like? There's a certain bonus in not knowing, maybe—Cinderella, princess, kitchen maid, mysterious enigmatic figure, pleasant, remote, aloof, obscure, warm, cold, bitter, sweet...

What goes for the girl on the bicycle goes for a lot of things:

Walking in the wind
Biting an apple
At a grave side
Washday
A rat in the cellar
Madame Miramar
Watching a spider consume a fly
Going down a slide
An old lady's parlour

On the roof
A ride in a pony and trap
Walking in the snow
At the Café des beaux arts
Empty station

These are random thoughts from my own experience, memories, moments of no particular significance to me at this moment, though, if I look at them very closely, I daresay I can find the significance there, the reason they came to mind, maybe even a pattern in their juxtaposition. But, for the present, let's just consider them as isolated fragments. Let's take one and write about it, just as the thoughts come to mind:

On the roof was a different world, a world of other roofs, a world where people walked like characters from old tales, where small dogs trotted unobserved. But a world also of surprise—the actual size of the chimney, but also roof slates as big as your arm. A world of angles and slopes that defied the feet. But especially a world of birds—startled by the intrusion of the wingless, they looked curiously suspicious like an acrobat who finds an amateur on his swing. They deferred judgment but waited for you to put a foot wrong.

Having looked through this later, I am tempted to rewrite it (it was written while students were writing themselves) or to choose something else. Nevertheless, I've decided to be honest and let it stand. Because it is honestly the first thoughts that came to mind. What could I do with it? I could rewrite it as a poem, possibly. I could use it as a piece to add to my collection of memories, moments from the past for an autobiographical novel I might one day get round to writing. I could use it for a short story. (See William Sansom's story about the boy who climbs the gas container[1]). But, principally, I need it here to illustrate the kind of ideas that for some reason are connected with the image "On the roof".

Students might jot down their own memories or ideas suggested by the above, and then choose one, or even take one from my list, if any seems appealing, and write freely about the ideas promoted by the main image. Having done that, discuss what you've written in terms of the ideas themselves, the nature of the language, and the

---

[1] "The Vertical Ladder" in *Selected Short Stories* (Penguin)

potential usefulness of the pieces as a poem or basis for a story, or anecdote or part of autobiographical novel.
SEE p 33 Reminiscence of Childhood, and also p 172.

A ROSE IS A ROSE IS A ROSE

An image which recurs again and again in Literature with symbolic force is the rose. As a symbol of love it is ubiquitous, from the great medieval poem *The Romance of the Rose* (see Chaucer's version) onwards. In Western thought it may be the equivalent of the lotus in Eastern thought as a symbol of perfection – a mystic centre, a symbol of some unattainable beauty; it is associated with the garden of Eros, with the paradise of Dante, with innocence (and perhaps also with sexual experience) in Eliot's "Burnt Norton":

Footfalls echo in the memory
Down the passage which we did not take
Towards the door we never opened
Into the rose-garden. My words echo
Thus in your mind.
But to what purpose
Disturbing the dust on a bowl of rose-leaves
I do not know.[1]

Shakespeare uses the image of the cankered rose for blighted or corrupted love, as does Blake in his strange, haunting and teasing poem "The Sick Rose":

O rose, thou art sick:
The invisible worm,
That flies in the night,
In the howling storm,

Has found out thy bed
Of crimson joy;
And his dark secret love
Does thy life destroy.

[1] l. 11-17 "Burnt Norton" *Four Quartets* (Faber)

See F. R. Leavis's detailed commentary in *Scrutiny* vol. XIII, No. 1, for suggestions about the significance of the rose and the "invisible worm" as some kind of brutal reality that corrupts innocence. (An extract is given on p 174.)

Another poet who found rich possibilities in the rose as a symbol was Yeats. In "Red Rose, proud Rose, sad Rose of all my days" he seems to use it as a symbol of beauty, eternal and unchanging, physical love, religion, his native country, intellectual beauty, as well as to represent subtle, less easily defined notions, which is of course the virtue of a good symbol.[1]

Students might jot down images and ideas, associations they make with the word ROSE and arrange the material into some kind of pattern as a poem, in free verse or as a concrete poem (see pp 14 and 135).

Here is the first rough draft of a poem written in these circumstances:

In the garden where the quiet rose waited
And old stems bridled with thorns
Where the rain fell in silent veils
And the red roses danced
Blood rose fell in flakes
The torn flesh of the rose lies bleeding
The blood torn flesh of the rose in the night

The still rose waits in the garden
Reaching the light

Find out all you can about the rose as an image in Literature. Look up references in *Brewer's Dictionary of Phrase and Fable,* and in *The Oxford Dictionary of Quotations.*

Try a similar thing with: lotus, bee, pearl, snake, bone, mandala, tiger...

[1]See W. B. Yeats "The Rose of the World", "The Rose of Peace", "The Rose of Battle", "The Rose Tree"

WORDS, WORDS, WORDS

Individual words exert a particular fascination on us; they lodge in the mind like thorns, to score and throb until we pull them out and examine or discard them. Or, to change the metaphor, they fall like seeds and penetrate, sending out roots to curl round other words, finally to put forth ideas. However, apart from the words we need to know and acquire familiarity with in our work— or for the purpose of exams, maybe— there are words that stick or attract or rub up against us for no other reason than that they are there, that they have a kind of gleam or lure, that their shape or sound is enticing even if we don't know their meaning. Here are a few words that have come into my consciousness recently, and for one reason or another seem to be stuck there:

lustrous fronds slaked nugatory patina snape plumbago
arcane felly mendacious veils integuments silver
lugubrious mumchance susurration

I could go on. Perhaps students will make up their own lists of words and then examine them and say why they think they've put them down (sound, meaning, metaphoric possibilities, etc). In my own case, I think many are words I've presumably come across in books and don't use very often; or I find I like the sound of the words (like lugubrious, and integuments); or perhaps even, the words, or some of them, seem to be useful words for metaphoric conjuction:

veils of silence, veils of thought, veils of light
fronds of sound, fronds of drifting thought
patinas of butterfly light, patinas of joy
enmeshed in obscure integuments of thought
susurration of insect wings on the afternoon stillness

I don't know that I'd ever use any of these in writing, although I might; they are more the result of a sort of private game one plays in the head while attending a boring meeting, or lecture. Nevertheless, there are possibilities for development there.

Quite often there's a right word to decribe what you want to say.

I'm not thinking only of the *mot juste* but of the kind of specific noun which is *the* word—nouns seem the most elusive of words. Here are some examples of the kind of thing I mean:

dottle felly sneck bevel bleb furl

Find some more and discuss them. Apart from their usefulness in that they have a particular meaning, what other quality do you think they have which might make them useful in, say, a poem?

Sometimes there is an appropriate word to describe someone's features, or physical appearance. In his *Writer's Notebook*[1] Somerset Maugham describes himself as "slightly prognathous". Now, there is no other single word I can think of that does the trick as well. You could say his lower jaw stuck out a little below his upper, but it seems clumsy; it might occur to you to say that he had a Hapsburg chin—but he didn't. Prognathous is the word. Here are some more—add to them.

exophthalmic	unipedal	glabrous
acromegalous	unguiculate	squamous

Of course, apart from using the rather ponderous words of classical origin, there are numerous other ways of effectively and evocatively describing features or appearance:

eyes pouched in sepia rings
flashing teeth like a piano keyboard
the placid face of a sandstone Buddha
face contorted like a bunched fist
ears which had he flapped them might well have
  lifted him off the ground
eyes like rust holes in the snow

One reporter described a famous comedian as having a face like a landslide. W. H. Auden was described as having a face like the bole of an ancient oak.

Students should make up some more. It's perhaps worth noting that it's a good deal easier to exaggerate oddities of feature than to convey distinctive or plain features neutrally. Try it.

OTHER SUGGESTIONS FOR WORK

1) Collect words that have been haunting you.
2) Look up words in dictionary beginning with particular letter and then make up a poem employing as many as you like.

[1] *A Writer's Notebook* (Penguin)

3) Collect some vogue words, eg situation, bad scene, take off, rip-off, etc. Use them in a parody (see p 178-9).
4) Collect words on particular themes, eg words for semi-precious stones: topaz, lapis lazuli, etc; or words for particular practical things: flange, lug, hasp,trivet, spacer, tundish. Make them into a concrete poem (see p 135).
5) Some group or collective terms have an odd, curious or slightly comic appeal: a wisp of snipe, a skulk of foxes, a nide of pheasants, a smuck of jellyfish, a paddling of ducks, a kindle of kittens, etc. These are accepted terms, but, of course, there's no reason why we can't make up our own, which is presumably how some of the above have come about. The language develops by invention, as when Dylan Thomas at the beginning of his essay "Holiday Memory"[1] offers us a mass of seaside images, most in the form of group terms:

> August Bank Holiday. A tune on an ice-cream cornet. A slap of sea and a tickle of sand. A fanfare of sunshades opening. A wince and whinny of bathers dancing into deceptive water. A tuck of dresses. A rolling of trousers. A compromise of paddlers. A sunburn of girls and a lark of boys. A silent hullabaloo of balloons.

   Students might like to try making up their own appropriate collective terms for, say: lipsticks, kidneys, sardines, pianos, pop-singers, television-sets, bicycles, beer-glasses, knickers, umbrellas, daffodils, guitars, fountain-pens, oranges, etc, etc.
6) A number of words characterizing the movements of creatures have long seemed appropriate: a horse *gallops,* a wolf *lopes,* a bear *lumbers,* etc; but there is no requirement to use only received expressions, and, in fact, the writing in a story may gain much of its descriptive energy from the colourful and novel way the writer has selected a word or expression in the context. Ted Hughes for example describes an otter which

   Gallops along land he no longer belongs to.[2]

   Consider some creature moving: a cat, thrush, beetle, bee, moth, tortoise, etc, either a pet, a bird flying, something real or imagined. Perhaps, looking out of the window, you can see some such creature. (First-hand experience is always best.) Try in a few

---

[1] *Quite Early One Morning* (Dent)   [2] "An Otter" in *Lupercal* (Faber)

sentences to capture the movement of the creature, however you like. When you've tried one, try another, perhaps using a different approach. If you are stuck, try to collect words for the precise description of the edgy movements of, say, an insect in contrast with the lumbering, more ponderous movements of, say, an elephant or cow or camel. (Is "ponderous" appropriate to a camel?)

7) Words in terms of both their sound and their associative qualities can create an impression of the bleak, the overpowering, or the exotic. Consider the following extract from "The Wreck of the Deutschland" by Gerard Manley Hopkins:

Into the snows she sweeps,
Hurling the haven behind,
The Deutschland, on Sunday; and so the sky keeps,
For the infinite air is unkind,
And the sea flint-flake, black-backed in the regular blow,
Sitting Eastnortheast, in cursed quarter, the wind;
Wiry and white-fiery and whirlwind-swivellèd snow
Spins to the widow-making unchilding unfathering deeps.

In Canto II of *The Rape of the Lock* (Pope) Ariel threatens the inattentive sylph with a variety of punishments for carelessness:

Gums and pomatums shall his flight restrain,
While clogg'd he beats his silken wings in vain:
Or alum styptics with contracting power
Shrink his thin essence like a rivell'd flower.

Jot down words which seem to you exotic, sharp, bitter, powerful, rugged, and then relate them to some particular mental picture: say, a North African Bazar or street market (see p 129-30), a tropical forest, a bleak mountainous region. Finally here's an extract from *Sir Gawain and the Green Knight,* a fourteenth-century poem from the North West of England, full of words of Scandinavian origin, and which somehow by its very tonal quality manages to convey a sense of the craggy, bleak wildness of the landscape of those times. I've modernized some of the words so that they are easier to read, but I've tried to preserve the sound of the original:

When the cold clear water fro the clouds shed
And froze ere it fall might to the fale[1] *earth*

[1] *Fale*—pale, faded

Near slain with the sleet he slept in his irons
More nights than enough in naked rocks,
There as clattering from the crest the cold burn[1] *runs*
And hanged high over his head in hard icicles

II l. 727-32

8) Whatever the quality of vocabulary (the sound, appearance, *colour* of the words, etc) that appeals to you, try a short piece of writing where that quality creates the effect.

RAIN

Just think of it—beating on the roof of a shed, lashing against windows, gurgling down gutters, spitting on asphalt, cascading over a downpipe, trickling slowly down a pane of glass, dripping imperceptibly a last few drops from a twig...and then, sunlight filtering through rain...

Try to think of as many manifestations of rain as you can. The ones I've listed are only ones you can see. You can *hear* rain, of course. You can also feel it—on your face, down your neck!

Consider being out in rain—on a bicycle, say, or walking bareheaded, or with an umbrella, swimming in a lake or in the sea in the rain, sheltering in a hut, in a tent...

Think of the street in the rain, rain on the leaves of trees, in a wood...

When you've got a reasonable collection of ideas which suggest rain in all its variety, arrange your ideas in some kind of appropriate form. You might begin every other line or every stanza of a poem, for instance, with "Rain falls...", and then go on to give examples; you might begin as I did with a storm, follow through the different stages and features of the falling rain, relaxing it until it is no more than a few drops, and finally have the sun breaking through; you might simply chart the patterns—and interesting thoughts they suggest—of rivulets of rain on a window-pane; or you might arrange your material in the form of a concrete poem. There's an example by the nineteenth-century French poet Guillaume Apollinaire in the Appendix p 173.

Write a short piece using one of the above as a starting point. Or consider some situation in which a description of the rain would be

[1]*burn*—stream

relevant, eg a storm at sea in an open boat or fishing trawler, climbing a mountain in the rain. Here's an extract from a novel by D. H. Lawrence:

> One afternoon in early October, feeling the seething rising to madness within her, she slipped out in the rain, to walk abroad, lest the house should suffocate her. Everywhere was drenched wet and deserted, the grimed houses glowed dull red, the butt houses burned scarlet in a gleam of light, under the glistening, blackish purple slates. Ursula went on towards Willey Green. She lifted her face and walked swiftly, seeing the colliery and its clouds of steam for a moment visionary in dim brilliance, away in the chaos of rain. Then the veils closed again. She was glad of the rain's privacy and intimacy.
>
> Making on towards the wood, she saw the pale gleam of Willey Water through the cloud below, she walked the open space where hawthorn trees streamed like hair on the wind and round bushes were presences showing through the atmosphere. It was very splendid, free and chaotic.
>
> Yet she hurried to the wood for shelter. There, the vast booming overhead vibrated down and encircled her, tree trunks spanned the circle of tremendous sound, myriads of tree-trunks, enormous and streaked black with water, thrust like stanchions upright between the roaring overhead and the sweeping of the circle underfoot.
>
> ...She turned under the shelter of the common, seeing the great veils of rain swinging with slow, floating waves across the landscape. She was very wet and a long way from home, far enveloped in the rain and the waving landscape...[1]

An open landscape in the rain can be very impressive, especially in rolling or hilly country. Notice how Lawrence creates the impression of immensity, power: "vast booming overhead vibrated down and encircled her," he says. One feels very much *in* that landscape and also very much that, although it has come out of Lawrence's imagination as he was writing it, he knows that experience, has observed it very carefully and with excitement, perhaps.

Students might make an effort to notice, or rather to absorb—because that is what Lawrence seems to have done—such experiences, not only rain in a semi-industrial landscape, but waves

[1]From *The Rainbow* (Heinemann/Penguin)

breaking over rocks, sun on slate roofs, etc—anything, in fact, which we tend to be fully aware of as children but notice less and less as we get older. As W. H. Davies says, we "have no time to stand and stare". It's a pity because our lives might be a lot richer, and, perhaps even, less complicated, if we did.

DETAIL II

Throughout the book a lot is said incidentally about the effective use of detail, and perhaps that is the way it should work in fiction: it should seem incidental. And yet the writer may have worked hard to get it just right, to give that touch of reality which engages our imagination: Mr Tench perfunctorily throwing the bit of stone at the vultures[1] or Justine hugging her hands under her armpits.[2] The writer may allow his selection of repeated detail to become something of almost symbolic importance, as when, for example, Harriet in *Where Angels Fear to Tread* mentions that she has lent Lilia her inlaid box ("lent, not given," she urges at one point). Several times Forster draws attention to this box and it becomes a symbol of Harriet's narrow-minded pettiness and her unswerving resolution. We scarcely notice in Patrick White's *The Tree of Man* that the rose trees flourish or wither and that these changes run parallel with the times of Amy's miscarriages and the birth of her children, and yet the detail is there to give point to the situation. We could hardly avoid noticing that the wind howls and the storm rages about Lear's head as it does within it. So there is a whole range of ways, some more significant than others, in which a writer might use detail. In a sense, detail ought only ever to be significant. There is no point in loading the story with detail that simply clutters. It has to give a sense of verisimilitude; or, perhaps, make a point about the character's mood; or say something about the character's life, or the events in the book. Students might like to reflect on those moments they can recall from books where the detail has stayed in their minds either because it seems "real" or because it is significant in the story

[1]See p 11 [2]See p 77

in some way. Below are a few that have come into my mind while writing this. Students will recognize some of them and argue about their significance:

Incident of the broken umbrella in *Sons and Lovers*
Bill Sykes being followed by his dog in *Oliver Twist*
Rosamund turning her head as Lydgate talks to her in *Middlemarch*
Powerful effect of the sun at the moment Meursault kills the Arab in *The Outsider*
Focus on the biscuit on the carpet at the moment Mrs Brigstock enters to find Fleda and Owen together in *The Spoils of Poynton*
Gerald compelling his mare to face the train at the level crossing in *Women in Love*
Repeated use of the detail of water in *A Portrait of the Artist as a Young Man*

Students then might like to make a note, for their own private use or for discussion, of detail from their own lives and experiences which they find memorable, or usable.

Below are some examples of detail which in a story might in some way be significant. Each is followed by comments on what the detail might be used to suggest.

1) Strong smell of disinfectant everywhere.

Might indicate someone obsessed with PURITY, cleanliness, morality. Someone trying to wipe out or reject living things, or vitality, etc. Cf. Mrs Ogmore-Pritchard in *Under Milk Wood*: "And before the sun comes in, mind it wipes its shoes..."

2) Hands carefully folded in her lap. An elegant pose. Contrived no doubt to show to advantage the long white fingers and the graceful line of the forearm.

HANDS FOLDED may be an indication of her cool superiority or her desire to appear superior or calm, or controlled, etc.

3) The vast sea of noisy chatter at whose brink he paused before plunging in and allowing himself to be driven along by it.

NOISE may indicate confusion, disorder, something he is anxious to avoid or refrain from involving himself with. Maybe a lively sea (vitality, moving life, etc) or the chaos of the human predicament, or just horror of people in the mass...

4) The lawn mown to within half an inch of the earth, the privet hedge trimmed precisely, the vegetables in exact rows, the flowers in rank according to height, season and hierarchical position in the floral calender; not an unofficial weed in evidence anywhere.

The ORDERED GARDEN frequently a symbol of ordered personality or desire for order, under attack from real, natural life. For example, in *Where Angels Fear to Tread* Mrs Herriton is sowing peas in careful rows when telegram arrives which will disrupt her life; she leaves the sowing and returns to find birds have eaten all the peas...

5) Chance incident—wall at side of house or in garden falls down, trees uprooted or struck by lightning, cat gets run over, etc.

All CHANCE INCIDENTS can be used simply or with subtlety and complexity to suggest some attitude or unspoken feeling of characters, or perhaps to symbolize chance nature of events. Examples: the incident of the dog falling from the aeroplane onto the roof as two people make love in Huxley's *Eyeless in Gaza;* the cat run over in Forster's *Howards End* used to indicate different reactions of occupants of the car; the scorpion killing the child in John Steinbeck's *The Pearl* indicates the vulnerability of the poor, but also shows how they have fallen into the clutches of something vicious and destructive.

Make up some more and note what you think they might be used to suggest in a story.

In your writing try to make your use of detail effective and relevant; but as a way of trying to get the whole business into perspective, and so that you don't fall into the trap of overdoing it on every conceivable occasion, you might like to try a parody of the kind of overdone writing I am suggesting you avoid, possibly using any or all (if you can manage it) of the ideas I've been considering.

SENSE OF ATMOSPHERE

It is possible to create a whole world on a bare stage with no props or few, and one or two people talking (eg *Waiting for Godot),* or perhaps not even talking at all *(Act Without Words*[1]*).* Sometimes in a novel or story only the dialogue is necessary; the mood and action are established through what the people say.[2] Sometimes the minimum of dialogue and a more detailed account of place and feeling creates the effect the writer wants. If you're writing a story or a novel, you obviously have to decide what's appropriate for the ideas you have; you may have to play around with ways of putting things, experiment with devices and so on. Here's a bit of dialogue:

A: Honestly, Julia, I waited for hours...
B: You knew there'd be a reason.
A: Obviously there's a *reason.* But how do I know what it is?
B: There's no need to be belligerent.
A: Belligerent? I didn't know I was being belligerent. I thought I was showing concern. Does that seem strange to you that I might be concerned...?

You might like to go on with it. Or leave it as it is. Whichever you decide, fill in the details—for example, where are they? (In a café, on the seashore, top of a skyscraper, basement, bedroom, aeroplane, car, etc.) Are they alone, or are there other people about, listening perhaps? What's the weather like? And is it important? What time of year, country, landscape, accent...? What are their backgrounds? Or is it better not to know? Who are they? The same age? Or different ages, old, young, dead...? How do they say what they say? Sorrowfully, angrily, petulantly, thoughtfully? How do they react to what each says to the other—hurt, annoyed, etc?

You may be filling in the details in your imagination just to give a sense of place, to make it realistic. Would it be appropriate to select details which would somehow enhance the scene in terms of colour, mood, etc? (See opening of *The Power and the Glory* p 11 this book.)

[1]Samuel Beckett *Endgame and Act Without Words* (Faber)

[2]See, for instance, the novels of Ivy Compton-Burnett

Fill in the fragment of dialogue with any detail you like. You may want to make it serious, moving, poignant, comic, or farcical, or even crazy. If you've tried one way, then have a go another way. You may find the bit of dialogue develops into a story; if that's the case then let it.

Having done that, make up a piece of dialogue of your own, or an interior monologue if you like, and then fill in the details. Alternatively, you might be disposed to make the dialogue itself convey the atmosphere. Or you might want your characters to be oblivious of their surroundings. How would you then describe the situation?

SOME THINGS TO DO

Wherever you are, in the street, with a group of people, waiting at a busstop, watching television, try to notice those aspects of the situation that make it what it is; it might be anything—somebody fumbling with the paper round a loaf of bread to get it into a shopping basket, removing the skin from a cup of coffee, characteristic way of holding a pencil, etc.

When you are reading, pause occasionally to note how the writer is getting his effect, perhaps with a bit of detail (the man reaches down to stroke the cat's head, the woman washes her hair, drying it vigorously with a towel), fragmentary dialogue (see Virginia Woolf's *Jacob's Room*, see p 57), description of what the characters are doing, or thinking, etc.

You might, if you are interested, start to make a collection of these observations for your notebook.

Finally here's a short extract from *The Eye of the Storm*[1] by Patrick White in which the famous actor Sir Basil Hunter has been invited back to the flat of an admirer of his, Mitty Jacka, who also happens to be a writer:

> He sat with a glass she had brought him, filled with something sweet, unacceptable, finally insidious, while she went about her animal business. Around him smouldered an upholstery of garnet plush, against panelling which looked like ebony, but couldn't have been. At least it was an ebony pedestal on which a figurine stood holding its curve under an ivory parasol. He found he had begun smiling into his sweet and fiery drink, while the voice of

[1] Jonathan Cape/Penguin

Mitty Jacka in the distance flung a few ritual 'darlings' to her animals.

He realised she was with him again on seeing her drop a piece of paper about the size of a visiting card into an urn on the shadowy outskirts of the room.

"What was that?" The drink inside him made him feel less brazen than spontaneous.

"Oh—an idea I might decide to use." She sounded unwilling, even a bit sour.

Then she was gone, followed by her anxious retinue. He continued sitting. Perhaps the smell of raw liver she left behind deterred him from investigating her 'idea'. Instead he waited: for what? His future as an actor of some importance no longer seemed relevant.

When she returned, not to settle—her behaviour suggested she might never do that, anyway during the hours of darkness—she freshened up his drink, more of which he had meant to refuse. As she moved about the room a cigarette she had lit for herself trailed its streamers of smoke, or described more elaborate arabesques as she stopped to look at and sometimes re-arrange objects she might have been seeing for the first time. She smoked so furiously that he was more drugged by her cigarette than drunk by whatever was in his glass.

From adding up a couple of her remarks he decided to risk her displeasure again. "I gather you write." Carefully composed, the words shot out of his mouth like a handful of independent marbles.

Discuss the effect of the detail in creating a sense of place and of atmosphere.

LETTERS

How many letters do you write in a lifetime? Thousands? None? Just think of the kinds of letters there are: begging letters, letters home from a battlefield, letters from an exile to his mistress, plea for clemency to the king, warnings, attacks, diplomatic missives, letters offering advice, rejecting it, letters of information, letters of condolence, of comfort, tragic letters. Discuss the kinds of letters there are, comic or serious, possibly doing a little research into letters from or to the great (see, for example, Dr Johnson's letter to Lord Chesterfield, Letters of John Keats, Dylan Thomas p 174, Letters to the Beatles, etc). Consider the kinds of letters people write to the Editors of newspapers, to the agony columns, letters of complaint to manufacturers or to employers (listen to Hoffnung's letter from a builder, who suffered a variety of injuries explaining his absence to his employer).

SUGGESTIONS FOR STUDENTS' WORK

1) Imagine a correspondence, comic or serious, between two characters: Anne Boleyn and Henry VIII, Shakespeare and Marlowe, Beethoven and Paul McCartney, etc.
2) Letter from Roman soldier stationed in Britain to his girlfriend in Italy.
3) Dead soldier writes to his general.
4) Girl in England writes to her lover in the Crimea, at Agincourt, Trafalgar, in India, etc.
5) South American explorer looking for lost city writes to his friend at home.
6) Dead man writes to his murderer.
7) Letter from Stanley Unwin to the Director General of the BBC offering his resignation as an engineer.
8) Letter from someone who doesn't speak the language very well asking for a room. Reply.[1]
9) Letter of complaint about a car, bicycle, guitar, record-player to the managing director of the firm who made it. "The tone arm of my record-player has already decapitated the cat, lacerated my wife's hand, drawn hideous zig-zag patterns on the only extant

[1]Listen to Hoffnung "At the Oxford Union" (BBC Records 157M)

copy in the world of a recording of the Hungarian dances by Brahms played by the composer himself..."

10) Letter of complaint about a lawn-mower that went out of control.
11) Letter home from an explorer who has encountered a tribe using an extraordinary musical instrument.
12) Letter from the Dragon to St George, Jack to the seed-merchant complaining about the beans, from some character in a book or play to the author who created him—"Dear William, Do you think it reasonable for me to wander about the stage in black all night, my stockings round my ankles and my shirt tails out—especially in this weather in a draughty castle inhabited by ghosts I am compelled to interview on the battlements, to allow myself to be abducted, fall into a grave, to say nothing about behaving embarrassingly over that mad idiot Ophelia, and ending up staggering about among the corpses of my family? I submit that this is a monstrous and insufferable imposition and remain respectfully, but tragically yours, Hamlet."

Choose any of the above, or one of your own devising, and compose it in the style that would be appropriate. If you try out a comic one, attempt another, more serious one, or perhaps one in which the problems of style are less important than the mood, eg letter to an unknown girl/boy...

THE NEWS

"Will John Smith, last heard of five years ago in the South of England, please go at once to the General Hospital, Leeds, where his mother is dangerously ill..."

How often have we heard a statement similar to this and wondered what is the story behind it, and what will be the outcome? Who is John Smith? Why has he not been heard of for five years? Is he out of the country? In jail? A success? Will he get the message? Will he act on it? Will his mother survive? Students might like to take this announcement and discuss the possibilities, perhaps working it into a short story.

The news probably provides one of the richest sources of raw material for any writer who wants to use it. Quite often it needs no more than a headline—"Dog bites man" excites little interest, but "Man bites dog" is not only news, it's an invitation to fantasize. The result might be a horror story, an SF story, or the heart-rending story of the breakdown in a beautiful relationship between one man and his dog! Students might like to collect, or devise similarly tempting headlines of their own and possibly write stories round them. Here are a few headlines taken from a newspaper over the last few days:

New York applauds its human fly
Gunmen free two children
Woman of 80 left £40,000
Poison found at School

I would suggest that students keep alert for any newspaper stories, items of interest, headlines, etc, and keep these in a book as source material from which to draw for stories. I have included a few brief stories from newspapers and magazines which might provide a challenge to students to discuss or write about, and perhaps that is all that is necessary. But students might find it helpful if I suggest ways in which these items might be tackled.

First of all, there is the story to work on and develop, which might be done in outline, as though it were a more extended version of the newspaper item itself. Sketch this out so that you have the sequence clearly in mind.

Then there is the detail, which is the life-blood of the story—the effect on Mr Smith of hearing the news, for example, his environment, or the eventual encounter between Mr Smith and his mother in hospital.

Also, there is the viewpoint to be considered. Do you want to tell the story from John Smith's point of view, in the first person perhaps? Or from the first/third-person viewpoint using the intimate "he" device (ie without necessarily using his name)? Or from some other angle? This will affect the style and tone of the writing. Suppose Mr Smith is a degenerate criminal serving out his time on Devil's Island, taking it into his head to escape to see his poor old mother (how did he hear about it incidentally?)—if it's from inside his head, it will have to convey the flavour of his mind. Or it might be told in the straight "dead-pan" fashion Hemingway was so fond of. Here is an example:

> They hanged Sam Cardinella at six o'clock in the morning in the corridor of the county jail. The corridor was high and narrow with tiers of cells on either side. All the cells were occupied. The men had been brought in for the hanging. Five men sentenced to be hanged were in the five top cells. Three of the men to be hanged were negroes. They were frightened. One of the white men sat on his cot with his head in his hands. The other lay flat on his cot with a blanket wrapped around his head.
>
> They came out on to the gallows through a door in the wall. There were seven of them including two priests. They were carrying Sam Cardinella. He had been like that since about four o'clock in the morning.
>
> While they were strapping his legs together two guards held him up and two priests were whispering to him. 'Be a man, my son,' said one priest. When they came toward him with the cap to go over his head Sam Cardinella lost control of his sphincter muscle. The guards who had been holding him up both dropped him. They were both disgusted. 'How about a chair, Will?' asked one of the guards. 'Better get one,' said a man in a derby hat.
>
> When they all stepped on the scaffolding back of the drop, which was very heavy, built of oak and steel and swung on ball bearings, Sam Cardinella was left sitting there strapped tight, the younger of the two priests kneeling beside the chair. The priest skipped back on to the scaffolding, just before the drop fell.[1]

Writing "dead-pan" is a salutory exercise for anybody interested in words, particularly if the theme is a potentially emotive one. It's worth noting here that although the writing seems spare, it is in fact only bare of commentary, of emotive words. There is a lot of detail—the man sitting on his cot with his head in his hands, the carrying of Cardinella, the smooth efficiency of the drop which runs on ball bearings, etc—and this focuses attention and allows the reader to make his own emotional responses, his own imagined picture of the scene.

Here are some headlines, fragments of news, and complete news items, which students might like to discuss in terms of story, situation, character or treatment:

---

[1]Ernest Hemingway "In Our Time" in *The First 49 Stories* (Jonathan Cape). Quoted in Poole and Shepherd *Impact* (Heinemann)

1) Mr Bill Brown, aged 67, and his wife, Olive, aged 70, have given up their fight to stay at the cottage which has been their home for twenty years.
2) Thomas Duggan, a building worker, was engaged in demolition work on a disused shop in Ealing when he discovered an old brown suitcase which contained some paintings. He took one to an upholsterer's shop and offered it as "old rubbish" for 5 shillings. It turned out to be Picasso's *Woman Weeping*...
3) A light aircraft with two passengers is missing in Alaska...
4) Girl locked in crypt tells of ordeal.
5) He told the Magistrates that if taken with the contraceptive pill it could produce strange effects.
6) Mary O'Brien returned to her family after an absence of seventeen years. "I never believed she was dead," said Mrs O'Brien.
7) A boy, aged 14, who was last seen on Monday climbing cliffs near Polperro, Cornwall, searching for bird's eggs, was last night presumed drowned after a search by police, coastguards and a helicopter failed to find any trace of him.
8) A priceless Renaissance painting of the Saints Peter and Paul and Zeno, part of a triptych by Andrea Mantegna completed in 1459, was stolen from the main altar in the presbytery of the Church of San Zeno Maggiore, in Verona, on Friday night. It was the latest of a series of thefts from unguarded churches in Northern Italy.
9) They were nearing the top when they became separated as the mist came down...
10) Titus, a Pyrenean sheepdog set out with his master, Daniel Gioria (23) of Pommiers-la-Plachette, Isèvres, for an expedition in the mountains of the Haute-Savoie. During the course of the climb the master but not the dog was buried in an avalanche of soft snow. Mr Gioria owes his life to the fact that the dog dug him out "furiously until he was uncovered". Together, in steadily worsening conditions, they turned for home. There was a moment when his owner had to abseil down a steep rock face, which was the only way to safety. So he installed the dog in a crevice in the rock at the top of the cliff and said: "Stay there! I'll come back for you." Soon after reaching the foot of the cliff, Mr Gioria, slightly frost-bitten and completely exhausted, was found by rescuers.

    "You've got to go and get my dog," he implored them. Three days later he himself was sufficiently recovered to accompany a party of six Alpine scouts who set out in search of Titus, and a distressed barking from the crevice told them that he had obeyed orders.

He was exactly where his master had left him, and very soon afterwards was back to safety again and none the worse for his adventure.

The Alpine scouts gave him a little bread to take the edge off his appetite, then strapped him to a harness and lowered him over the cliff. In the valley, there awaited a vet, who gave him a dose of vitamins and a bowl of soup, and his master wept, unashamed of his tears.

The dog trotted home under his own steam at the head of the party—a national hero.[1]

CHARACTER INTERACTION JOURNEY

Why is it that there are so many plays, novels, films, in which the setting is a railway carriage, an aeroplane, long-distance coach, or ship? Can you think of specific instances?[2]

One fairly clear attraction for the writer is that the idea offers an opportunity of bringing together a variety of disparate characters with different social backgrounds and personalities, all in a confined space, for a brief period of time. Since they can't immediately get away, there is the possibility of menace, of relationships developing or becoming exacerbated by antagonisms; and since the vehicle is subject to mechanical or other failure or, perhaps, at the mercy of the elements, there is the possibility of action and danger. Also, of course, there is the journey itself. Why are the people making it at all? Consider the different motives and reasons.

Suggest a group of characters and find reasons for their presence, the purpose of their journey, etc. Invent backgrounds for them. They might be a bizarre collection: a circus clown, a safe-breaker, pop-singer, window-cleaner, snake-charmer, etc. They might be a collection of like characters: business-men on a trip, musicians belonging to a symphony orchestra, members of a women's guild.

---

[1]From *The Guardian* (Nesta Roberts)

[2]B. Traven *The Death Ship,* Richard Hughes *In Hazard,* Neville Shute *No Highway,* B. S. Johnson *Trawl,* Evelyn Waugh *The Ordeal of Gilbert Pinfold,* John Steinbeck *The Wayward Bus,* Graham Greene *Stamboul Train,* E. M. Forster "The Celestial Omnibus".

They might represent a cross-section of the community.

Then consider how to handle the idea. Is it to be realistic? Perhaps the characters simply reveal something of their ordinary lives. Perhaps one behaves oddly, or dangerously, or neurotically, or, say, has a gun and threatens the others. What happens?

Perhaps they suddenly open up to each other because of some external threat. Recently there was a breakdown on a tube train during the intense heat of the summer. People were locked together in a carriage. One happened to be a reporter who described the scene later. Some people lost their temper, somebody broke a window, somebody fainted. But whereas before, nobody had said a word to anybody else, when they were finally rescued all were talking freely, telling each other about their lives. People had thrown off their cloak of reserve, they had become a social group. No doubt they went back to their old ways next day. But for the time being...

The journey can also be a metaphysical journey: a journey of life, a journey which represents some kind of paradigm of reality where events, and perhaps even people, are symbolic. Think of Ibsen's *Peer Gynt,* Anouilh's *Point of Departure,* Bunyon's *The Pilgrim's Progress.*

There are a number of forms such an idea might take, depending on the treatment you find most appealing. A play for radio, for instance, film scenario, short story. But perhaps the simplest way, especially if you are not certain, is to note down ideas for your characters and begin to sketch out the plan for a story. Some writers prefer to write the story to find out what happens, so that the story itself becomes a process of exploration.

SOME POSSIBILITIES

1) Four people come together: a judge, a philosopher, a general, a poet. Discuss their attitudes to life. Opportunity for intellectual exploration as well as character exploration.
2) Five people from different walks of life: housewife, millionaire, actor, model, farm labourer. Attitudes to food, art, revolution, religion, life...
3) Four characters from history or literature find themselves on a ghost train...
4) Plane crash in snow, mountains, etc. Six people survive, the rest are dead...
5) Plane crash in desert. How do people survive?
6) Holiday car, or coach, or jeep on long cross-continental journey.

Get lost. In reality? Or lost in different world...

7) Character gets out of train on station in darkness. Train pulls out without him...
8) Yachtsman whose boat has capsized after hours in the sea is picked up by strange ship with strange crew or passengers...
9) Three astronauts in space capsule. Where? Problems?
10) Two or three passengers in basket of ballon drifting... where? (Over sea, out of control, lost, over desert, jungle, unknown terrain...)

CHARACTER I

Two discussion points:

1. What constitutes character in a work of fiction?
2. What constitutes character in a real person? How do you define it?

Clearly the first very much depends on the second. In order to describe someone you know, you choose those attributes, traits, mannerisms, attitudes you can readily identify, and if you are subtle or the character of the person you are trying to describe is elusive, then you may have to refine or modify your description by attempting to express these subtleties.

Consider the kind of features that might help to convey a character. Discuss.

One possible approach is to think of the character's overall attitudes to life, his philosophy, the kind of attitudes he adopts to money, perhaps, or position, what he thinks important. A lot of this would reveal the *type* of person he is. If he staggers onto the stage shouting "Down with the Bureaucrats, the opposers of liberty! Up with individualists!", then we get some idea of his attitudes, unless he is being ironic, and that may tell us more.

There's also what he does. If he beats up an old lady in the street, steals her handbag, kicks her shopping and then smashes her hand when she tries to reach out to protect the small child with her... An obvious example? Well, think of a subtler one. Man receives a letter, he crumples it and throws it away, or tears it into fragments—what might that tell us? Something about the letter, probably, but it might also tell us something about the man.

There are also idiosyncratic features: the man has a habit of rubbing his chin with his forefinger extended; the woman twists a strand of hair around a finger; an upper lip twists down to conceal some false teeth; a child rubs an eye which is watering, picks the scab on a knee.

There are also idiosyncratic movements or sounds or words: a man keeps using the substitute "whatsername"—"We went down the whatsername Saturday and saw the whatsername, football match, and whatsername was there with the whatsername, mascot..."; the woman draws in her upper lip nervously, taps her teeth with a pencil, removes her glasses thoughtfully in a gesture which proclaims her intellectuality; the man on the top of the bus picks his nose furtively; the speaker spreads his hands expansively across his waistcoat, jabs a forefinger, etc. Think of others.

Dress is another feature which might identify the person in the mind of the reader (think of Mr Pickwick, Mr Micawber, Fagin, Captain Cuttle, the Artful Dodger). But features of dress may convey a little more of the character, tell us something of a man's attitudes: "A portly man in his middle-fifties with very tight blue jeans which drew attention to the overlapping paunch, block-heel shoes and long straggling grey hair from the sides of his head, the crown of which was quite bald..."; "A perky woman in her mid-forties wearing a two-piece tweed suit with a trilby hat and a velvet tie, and smoking a cheroot..."

And then there is the sense of a person in a particular place: for example, the young man strolling along the shop-windows, occasionally looking in, bracing his shoulders, pretending to look at the goods on display while in fact consumed by his own reflection, trying to determine whether the back of his head really does look like that of Steve McQueen, whether his smile has anything in common with Paul Newman's. In the opening of her novel *Sweet William*[1] Beryl Bainbridge has a young woman saying goodbye to her lover at the airport. She sees her distorted reflection in the chrome of the cigarette machine, and later she notices another distorted reflection of herself. What might such observations tell us about the character?

In the light of the above discuss and note any aspects of character

[1]Fontana

you can think of which might help convey the sense of a person.

Think of a real character you know, or have observed. Try to re-create in your imagination the attributes of this person, their mode of speech, nature, idiosyncracies, gestures, existence in a particular place at a particular time. To refer again to Beryl Bainbridge's novel, there is a moment when the heroine is thinking of the new man who has become her lover and she notices the area of flesh between the hair on his neck and his jumper. That little detail helps to fix the girl and the man and her feeling for him very clearly and succinctly in the reader's imagination.

Find examples from your reading, discuss and make notes on how the effect is created.

SEE pp 11, 57ff, 68ff, 106ff, 112ff, 129ff

WHAT'S IN A NAME

If you write a story in which your main character is called Lizzie Scraggit, it seems to me you are saying something about the character, something different from what you'd be saying if you decided to call her Eleanor Langridge. Certain names have overtones and you hope to dispose your reader, maybe set up certain stock response expectations, by the names you give your characters: your tough north-country working-class lad is called Ben Arkwright, visiting the house of a group of Hampstead intellectuals with names like Annunciata and Jocelyn. The name of Patrick White's hero in *The Tree of Man* is Stan Parker. Apart from having a kind of Australian ordinariness about it, it has important symbolic associations relevant to the book: Stan is the Old English word for stone, Parker has associations with gardens, with land transformed into parkland, associations with the Garden of Eden, perhaps, which are exploited particularly towards the end of the book. Stan's wife is called Amy (Fr. beloved), their son is called Ray, which turns out to be ironical. Golding calls the hero of his book *Pincher Martin* Christopher which means "Christ bearer" and this is perhaps both ironic, in view of Christopher's character, and, in another way, an indication of his function as Everyman/Prometheus; but his naval nickname is interesting in that it illustrates Christopher's character as a stealer—he takes what belongs to others, particularly from his friend Nathaniel ("gift of god"). Think of the qualities associated with names in Emily Brontë's novel *Wuthering Heights*: the name of the place itself is in contrast with the gentler sounding Thrushcross Grange, while the names of the characters Heathcliff and Hareton seem contrasted with those of the Lintons. Think of the names of characters in other books and plays, etc, that you know. What sort of qualities do you associate with their names?

Writers have always used names because of their associations, of course—think of Madame Eglentyne, Chaucer's Prioress; Andrew Aguecheek, Toby Belch and Malvolio in *Twelfth Night*; not to mention the names in Dickens: Fang, Heep, Magwitch, Bumble.

People often seem to have names appropriate or wildly inappropriate to their professions: a famous firm of estate agents in the Midlands glories in the names of Doolittle and Dally. What names can you think of that would be appropriate or inappropriate to a firm of solicitors, painters and decorators, butchers, doctors, accountants, dentists, etc?

Other people who seem to have names which are intended to characterize them are pop-stars (Colvin Starlight, Toni Lametta, Wayne Tinsell), or filmstars (Steve Hemisphere, Brad Wayne, Gloria— —?). But, of course, fashions change and the names just suggested are placeable in the 'fifties and 'sixties (which of course might make a point in your story).

Students might consider a suitable setting for a novel or a play or film scenario involving a group of characters from different walks of life—a boat cruise might be a suitable situation. Who would be the passengers? Give them names and backgrounds. Here are a few to start you off:

Hiram B. Allworthy, a purveyor of religious tracts for an evangelical order
A Middle-Eastern merchant, Costas Eugenides
A tough, heavy-drinking, gambling private eye
A glamorous actress of the 'fifties
A country vicar and his wife from Rutland
A young Frenchwoman novelist
A degenerate English aristocrat
A rich widow from Budleigh Salterton and her young companion
A couple of ballroom dancing champions
A concert pianist, etc, etc.

Once you've begun, you might become interested in the characters, the reason for their presence on the ship, the possibilities of intrigue or adventure, action, death; or simply you might feel you have created a setting for a group of stories after Chaucer or Boccaccio.

Keep a look-out for interesting names and names that seem to have particular qualities or associations and make a note of them in your commonplace book.

CHARACTER II

As we have seen, there are various ways to describe people (p 102). Their names even may tell us something. Dickens often describes the appearance of a character in great detail, and from that we learn something of the character's personality. Joyce tells us what people are like by entering their heads. Henry James shows us the subtle ideas and thoughts which motivate a character's behaviour.[1] Lawrence tries to demonstrate the amorphous, unformed, essential nature of the person, the feelings that precede thought.[2]

Students might like to try their hands at re-creating a character, someone they know or someone they have invented, in one or all of the ways mentioned above (appearance, interior thoughts, description of thoughts, evocation of deeper, unformed feelings, etc).

But there is also the question of technique, the mode in which you might attempt to convey character. For some people the visual impact is very strong. The lines in someone's face, flowers in a rose-bowl on a table by the window, hands ringed, resting on the lap: note the effect of the visual images in this extract from Eliot's "Portrait of a Lady"[3]:

> *Now that lilacs are in bloom*
> *She has a bowl of lilacs in her room*
> *And twists one in her fingers while she talks.*
> *'Ah, my friend, you do not know, you do not know*
> *What life is, you who hold it in your hands';*

---

[1]See Henry James *The Turn of the Screw* or *The Spoils of Poynton* (Penguin)
[2]D. H. Lawrence "The Blind Man" in *England my England* (Penguin)
[3]In *Collected Poems* (Faber)

(Slowly twisting the lilac stalks)
'You let it flow from you, you let it flow,
And youth is cruel, and has no remorse
And smiles at situations which it cannot see.'
I smile, of course,
And go on drinking tea.

Try a piece of writing—free verse or prose—which captures the visual impression of a person in a room, perhaps someone you've gone to visit: grandfather, aunt, old Headmaster, famous poet, once beautiful actress, etc.

Think how effective the radio can be without directly visual images (although, of course, it may evoke visual images in the listener). A child or young girl, say, goes to visit an old person. Conversation is sporadic; there are long silences in which one can hear flies, or bees buzzing, and an occasional bird, the clock ticking, etc. The sense of the place of the person, perhaps of the immensity of time past, might be conjured up in this way. Suppose in the vacation you go to see someone very old—in a hospital bed, say, or in a room in a large old house with a vast garden, or in an old people's home, or in a high-rise flat, etc. Decide on the location and on the person and the kind of thing he or she is preoccupied with or remembers (pigeon-flying, football matches, the music hall, a ball, Paris in the Spring, etc), and then imagine it as a radio or sound play. Write it out with directions for sound, pauses, effects, etc. It is likely that the mood of such a piece will be one of introspection. (See "Imago" p 176)

By contrast, try something more outgoing, more boisterous, perhaps. Or a contrast between two people—one large and blustery, one small, dry, or birdlike. Here's an extract from a story by Dylan Thomas:

> I was staying at the time with my uncle and his wife. Although she was my aunt, I never thought of her as anything but the wife of my uncle, partly because he was so big and trumpeting and red-hairy and used to fill every inch of the hot little house like an old buffalo squeezed into an airing cupboard, and partly because she was so small and silk and quick and made no noise at all as she whisked about on padded paws, dusting the china dogs, feeding the buffalo, setting the mousetraps that never caught her; and oncc she sleaked out of the room, to squeak in a nook or nibble in the hayloft, you forgot she had ever been there.[1]

[1]From *A Prospect of the Sea* (Dent)

How does Thomas get his effects? Examine the imagery and discuss what you notice about it.

Here's a poem by Gillian who was aged 13 when she wrote it:

A Gardener drinking Tea

Gratefully gulping his hot cup of tea,
He belches and chokes,
And paddles the spoon round the edge of the cup
While he snatches a smoke.
As he rubs his cold nose on the sleeve of his coat
He sniffs, loosely and loud,
And, yawning, leans back on his damp, wooden seat,
With his grizzled head bowed.[1]

SUGGESTIONS

1) Collect some pictures, perhaps from newspapers or magazines. Describe the person in the photo or pictures in visual terms in as much detail as you can; then try to re-create what sort of person you think is depicted and what his or her life might be like.
2) Look at pictures of a man digging, woman pegging out washing, scissors-grinder, skier, ploughman, etc. Choose one and give a brief account in free verse, such as that by Gillian, above.
3) Listen to "Samuel Goldenburg and Schmuyle" from Mussorgsky's *Pictures at an Exhibition.* Try to characterize these two.
4) Listen to some music by an instrumentalist, pop singers, a lead guitarist, harpsichordist, etc. Try to create in words the impression they make. Possible ways: straightforward, or ironic prose description as it might appear in a newspaper report, or in a novel: formal poem as appropriate, eg Sonnet of Scarlatti at the Harpsichord, Sydney Bechet Plays, The Voice of Dory Previn, etc; typographical poem to suggest performer and sounds he/she makes.

[1]From *Young Writers Young Readers* (Hutchinson)

TIMES OF DAY

The stillness of dawn when only a few leaves cling trembling to the twigs, and the day has not yet stirred to the noise of movement of birds, people, traffic; when a single sound—the dropping of an enamel mug, for example—disturbs the universe for a second, and then leaves it as it was, suspended in silence, perfect stasis. The cold of the morning when people are drawn within themselves, the last drop of water from the hair stings the neck and reminds that day is opening up. The bridge between that silent immobility and the day...

The morning before the world is awake. I suppose we are all aware of it sometimes, although perhaps reluctantly. Think of the first venture out on a farm—the clatter of a bucket seems to echo across the landscape acres away. In the town, those first footsteps on the pavement to the bus stop. The vapour of breath on the air. A man waiting moves from one foot to another, collar turned up, hands deep in pockets.

What other images do you associate with the early morning, the break of day? The light perhaps? (Ted Hughes has a poem in which he refers to the "iron light" at this time of day.) Sounds of running water from a tap, sound of a toothbrush? The air—cold and undisturbed? Absence of traffic? Milk churns? Before the factory starts up? Write some down. Then think of some particular morning you remember vividly. When you've written a sketch of it, try another draft to improve on it.

Some students might prefer a more colourful approach. Aurora was goddess of the dawn. According to ancient writers, she "drew back the purple curtains of the dawn", was "saffron-robed", and "dispelled the darkness with her morning light". Aurora married a mortal called Tithonus for whom she secured eternal life. Unfortunately she failed to gain for him eternal youth, so he became older and older, while every day she was renewed with the dawn. Some writers (see Ovid's *Metamorphoses*[1], Tennyson's "Tithonus", etc) depict them in mansions of the heavens through which drift veils of

[1]Translated by Mary M. Innes (Penguin)

dawning, etc. If you find the rich exotic imagery of the myth appealing, perhaps you might write a poem or story about it, using your dawn as a starting point.

In her delightful story *Tom's Midnight Garden*[1] Philippa Pearce describes Tom getting up in the middle of the night to go out into the magic garden:

> The green of the garden was greyed over with dew; indeed, all its colours were gone until the touch of sunrise. The air was still, and the tree shapes crouched down upon themselves. One bird spoke; and there was a movement when an awkward parcel of feathers dislodged itself from the fir-tree at the corner of the lawn, seemed for a second to fall and then at once was swept up and along, outspread, on a wind that never blew, to another, farther tree: an owl. It wore a ruffled, dazed appearance of one who has been up all night.

This dead, silent time of night, just before the first glimmerings of day might provide a beginning for a story. First of all, you need to decide on the place (town, country, forest, suburb, etc), whether the story is in the present or in the past, from the viewpoint of some human or animal in the story, or from some objective, omnipotent viewpoint.

Morning, too, has its qualities. We all know the dreary rainy or drizzling morning when you go to school or college or work and your things are damp, your shoes sodden, the smell of wet wool in your nostrils; or those foggy mornings when you arrive at a place and everything seems subdued (see p 47) as though cocooned in cotton-wool. Or think of the morning which is all sun and brightness and even inanimate things seem to be smiling. Here's a rather nicely indulgent poem by Laurie Lee celebrating such a morning:

Such a morning it is when love
leans through geranium windows
and calls with a cockerel's tongue.

When red-haired girls scamper like roses
over the rain-green grass,
and the sun drips honey.

When hedgerows grow venerable,
berries dry black as blood,
and holes suck in their bees.

---

[1]OUP paperback

Such a morning it is when mice
run whispering from the church,
dragging dropped ears of harvest.

When the partridge draws back his spring
and shoots like a buzzing arrow
over grained and mahogany fields.

When no table is bare,
and no breast dry,
and the tramp feeds off ribs of rabbit.

Such a day it is when time
piles up the hills like pumpkins,
And the streams run golden.

When all men smell good,
and the cheeks of girls
are as baked bread to the mouth.

As bread and beanflowers
the touch of their lips,
and their white teeth sweeter than cucumbers.[1]

Think of the noise and the clatter, the colour, the variety and *vividness* of a sunny morning in summer or spring. Perhaps you could use this as the beginning of a story or autobiographical poem or novel.

CREPUSCULAR—an unusual word for twilight, which derives from the latin *crepusculum,* creeper. Think of some other words associated with evening: gloaming, dusk, etc.

Choose an occasion, a place, a time of year, eg: late afternoon, by the fire, with the light failing, in a house in the late nineteenth century; a journey through a rocky landscape, night drawing in, etc. Describe the atmosphere, the essential quality of the light, sound, the *feel* of the moment.

MUSIC

Benjamin Britten "Sea Pictures" from *Peter Grimes*
Delius "Song before Sunrise"
Grieg "Morning" from *Peer Gynt*
Debussy "Les sons et les parfums tournent dans l'air du soir" from 1st book *Preludes*

---

[1]"Day of these Days" in *The Sun my Monument* (Hogarth Press)

SURVIVORS

Most of us feel that we could manage to survive in difficult conditions. What sort of conditions might make it necessary? Make a note of some: air crash in snow-covered mountains, or in the desert or jungle; a new Ice Age; a terrible world war or atomic disaster; some sudden failure of the materials—food, perhaps, or metal, or energy—that we depend on.

What would one need in order to survive? Well, food, obviously, a place to live, some implements. Consider the possibilities. Robinson Crusoe did pretty well on his desert island because he had the shipwreck to plunder. Suppose you were not so fortunate: the lone survivor of an aircrash, for example, in the jungle or vast tract of uninhabited desert. How long, for instance, can one survive without water? A glider pilot who lost his way in the Australian desert managed to keep alive for several days by conserving the water in his body, not moving about—or only very little, when most of the sun had gone. Normally, a couple of days is about the limit in such terrible conditions, because of the loss of salt as well as moisture.

Choose one situation which you find challenging, and consider the problems and how you might overcome them, either alone or with a companion. Then concentrate on one particular problem, such as, say, fishing, lighting a fire or making a knife, in as much detail as you can imagine.

Here is an extract from a story by Jack London.[1] The man is a newcomer to the Yukon, and has unwisely gone out alone with a dog in the intense cold in order to return to a camp. He succeeds in lighting a fire, but he chooses to build it near a tree and eventually the snow on one of the branches thaws and puts out his fire. He panics and tries to light another, but the cold is so intense that his fingers are numb:

> He made a new foundation for a fire, this time in the open, where no treacherous tree could blot it out. Next he gathered dry grasses and tiny twigs from the high-water flotsam. He could not bring

[1] "To Build a Fire" in *The Call of the Wild and Selected Stories* (Signet)

his fingers together to pull them out, but he was able to gather them by the handful. In this way he got many rotten twigs and bits of green moss that were undesirable, but it was the best he could do. He worked methodically, even collecting an armful of the larger branches to be used later when the fire gathered strength. And all the while the dog sat and watched him, a certain yearning wistfulness in its eyes, for it looked upon him as the fire provider, and the fire was slow in coming.

When all was ready, the man reached in his pocket for a second piece of birch bark. He knew the bark was there, and, though he could not feel it with his fingers, he could hear its crisp rustling as he fumbled for it. Try as he would, he could not clutch hold of it. And all the time, in his consciousness, was the knowledge that each instant his feet were freezing. This thought tended to put him in a panic, but he fought against it and kept calm. He pulled on his mittens with his teeth, and threshed his arms back and forth, beating his hands with all his might against his sides. He did this sitting down, and he stood up to do it; and all the time the dog sat in the snow, its wolf brush of a tail curled around warmly over its forefeet, its sharp wolf ears pricked forward intently as it watched the man. And the man, as he beat and threshed with his arms and hands, felt a great surge of envy as he regarded the creature that was warm and secure in its natural covering.

After a time he was aware of the first faraway signals of sensation in his beaten fingers. The faint tingling grew stronger till it evolved into a stinging ache that was excruciating, but which the man hailed with satisfaction. He stripped the mitten from his right hand and fetched forth the birch bark. The exposed fingers went quickly numb again. Next he brought out his bunch of sulphur matches. But the tremendous cold had already driven the life out of his fingers. In his effort to separate one match from the others, the whole bunch fell in the snow. He tried to pick it out of the snow but failed. The dead fingers could neither touch nor clutch. He was very careful. He drove the thought out of his freezing feet, and nose, and cheeks, out of his mind, devoting his whole soul to the matches. He watched, using the sense of vision in place of that of touch, and when he saw his fingers on each side the bunch, he closed them – that is, he willed to close them, for the wires were down, and the fingers did not obey. He pulled the mitten on the right hand, and beat it fiercely against his knee. Then, with both mittened hands, he scooped the bunch of matches, along with much snow, into his lap. Yet he was no better off.

After some manipulation he managed to get the bunch between the heels of his mittened hands. In this fashion he carried it to his mouth. The ice crackled and snapped when by a violent effort he opened his mouth. He drew the lower jaw in, curled the upper lip out of the way, and scraped the bunch with his upper teeth in order to separate a match. He succeeded in getting one, which he dropped on his lap. He was no better off. He could not pick it up. Then he devised a way. He picked it up in his teeth and scratched it on his leg. Twenty times he scratched before he succeeded in lighting it. As it flamed he held it with his teeth to the birch bark. But the burning brimstone went up his nostrils and into his lungs, causing him to cough spasmodically. The match fell into the snow and went out.

The old-timer on Sulphur Creek was right, he thought in the moment of controlled despair that ensued: after fifty below, a man should travel with a partner.

Notice how the author takes every single bit of detail and explores it, moving step by step through the processes that involve the man.

Your own writing might be a bit of material for a story. In London's story the central matter is the man's attempt to light the fire. If you need a framework use a title such as "The Last Day"; your character finally reaches safety, having been involved, perhaps, in some travel disaster. "The Last Day" relates instances which indicate the nature of the adventure. London never names his character; he refers to him simply as "the man". Consider the effect of this. Decide whether you want to give your character a history, or do you want to keep him anonymous? This at least enables you to concentrate on the problems confronting him.

For those interested in reading in the area there are some fascinating stories. The following are suggestions for follow-up material or material for further discussion:

James Vance Marshall *Walkabout* (Penguin)
Patrick White *Voss* (Penguin)
James Canaway *Sammy Going South* (Penguin)
J. M. Ballantyne *Coral Island* (Blackie)
William Golding *Lord of the Flies* (Faber), *Pincher Martin* (Faber)
Edith Bone *Seven Years Solitary* (Pan)
Geoffrey Household *Rogue Male* (Penguin)

THE INTERROGATION SCENE

We've probably all been questioned sharply at some time so that we feel threatened, interrogated—at school over some minor misdemeanour, about some work neglected; so we know the feeling. Perhaps this is one reason why court-room and interrogation scenes are so popular in books, and especially on the stage. And, of course, it's all the better if the poor victim with whom we identify can come out on top and denounce his persecutors in an impassioned and thunderously rhetorical defence of his own individuality and innocence, on behalf of liberty and the general good. Think, for instance, of the powerful scenes in Bernard Shaw's *Saint Joan,* John Osborne's *Luther* and *Subject of Scandal,* Ibsen's *Enemy of the People.*

Perhaps the more menacing and disturbing situation is that of the interrogation, because it is conducted behind closed doors, possibly with the threat of torture and the demoralizing fear that the victim's suffering and heroic denunciations or resistance will never come to light. Again, this is a popular and compelling situation. Think of the opening scenes of Geoffrey Household's *Rogue Male,* Bolt's *A Man for All Seasons,* Brecht's *Galileo.* One of the most disturbingly extended series of interrogations, a study of interrogation in itself, is that in Arthur Koestler's *Darkness at Noon,* in which the old-guard revolutionary Rubashov, who has put many behind bars himself, is at last brought into custody and interrogated. Koestler examines the whole process of introspection and the psychological readjustment of his convictions by the victim in the course of interrogation.

Students might like to think of and discuss other examples in books or films or plays: the court-room scene in Herman Wouk's *The Caine Mutiny,* for example; the symbolic representation of interrogative threat in Kafka's *The Trial;* the process of the disintegrating will to resist in Orwell's *Nineteen Eighty-Four.* Or perhaps they might concentrate on real situations: the trials of Dreyfus, Daniel and Synaevsky, Bukovsky, Roger Casement, the MacCarthy hearings. Apart from these, students might like to research a little into earlier history, eg: Sir Thomas Wyatt, Lady Jane Grey, Raleigh, Edith Caval, etc. Here, for example, is an extract from the 1137AD entry to the Peterborough Chronicle[1] freely translated into modern English:

> Then King Stephen came to England and called a gathering at Oxford, and there he took Bishop Roger of Salisbury and Alexander Bishop of Lincoln and the Chancellor Roger and his "nephews", and put them all in prison until they had given up their castles. When the traitors saw that he was an easy-going man and did not apply justice properly they did all manner of evil things. They had made oaths to him and went back on their word, for every nobleman fortified his castles and held them against him and moreover they filled the land with fortresses. They greatly oppressed the poor people with castle building. And when the castles were built they filled them with evil men. Then they took the people they thought had anything worth having, both by night and by day, poor men and women, and put them in prison for gold and silver, and tortured them endlessly, and never were martyrs so afflicted as they were. They hanged people by their feet and smoked them with foul smoke. They hanged others by their thumbs or by their heads and hung mail shirts on their feet. They put knotted strings about their heads and twisted them and cut through to their brains. They put them in dungeons where there were toads and snakes and left them to die. Some they put in a *crucethus,* that is a very narrow, short and shallow chest full of sharp stones, and pressed them in until they broke their bones. In many of the castles there were head-bands and halters—chains which two or three men would have enough to do to bear one, and they fastened it to a beam and put the sharp iron collar about a man's throat so that he might move no way, neither sit nor lie nor sleep, but had to bear all that iron. Many thousands they punished with hunger. I can not nor am I able to describe all the suffering and all the torments they caused to poor men of this land, and that lasted 19 winters while Stephen was king, and it was ever worse and worse.

SUGGESTIONS FOR WORK

1) Take one of the above situations from history and research it. Then write a story or short play on the basis of your material.
2) Dialogue: child accused of theft by teacher, or someone in authority. Did he do it? (See *The Winslow Boy* by Terence

[1] The Anglo-Saxon Chronicle

Rattigan for a good interrogation scene by an attorney.)

3) Interrogation scene in cell. Decide on a situation, eg during a war, or in peace-time, espionage or criminal charge, in England or some remote country, etc.
4) Court scene: exchanges between some historical character (eg Galileo, Raleigh, etc) or some character of your own invention (pilot accused of negligence, someone accused of murder, etc) and the accusers.

INCARCERATION

People have been shackled by arms, legs, neck and waist to walls, floors and stakes, suspended in cages, put in boxes, iron masks and iron "maidens", chained to shelves, buried in holes for their beliefs, because of their scientific views, their imagination, their curiosity, and for nothing more than their kindness to others. Their seems no limit to man's ingenuity in devising means to incarcerate his fellows. A visit to almost any castle dungeon will probably do more to evoke a sense of what it is like to be cooped up, confined and cribbed, than any amount of verbal picturing. A walk across the Bridge of Sighs in Venice where victims saw their last light of day conjures up awful feelings of the despair such people must have felt. At the castle in Ferrara there is a dungeon, which can only be reached by a very low tunnel (one has to stoop to move forward at all), where the Duke imprisoned and killed his wife and the man he took to be her lover.[1] The Fortress of Loches is a warren of cells of various kinds and sizes, from which it was virtually impossible to escape. Ludovic the Moor (Count Sforza), Leonardo's patron who was captured by the French, was imprisoned in the Fortress of Loches for eight years (1500–08) and on his release died. It is said that when he walked into the sunlight, it was too bright and he died from the effect of this sudden emergence into daylight.

[1]Not Browning's famous Last Duchess (q.v.) who was in fact the fourteen-year-old Lucrezia de Medici, wife of Alfonso II, but Parisina Malatesta duchess of Niccolo III (1393–1441). Niccolo had numerous bastard sons, one of whom, Ugo, he is supposed to have seen in a mirror behaving amorously with Parisina, as a result of which he inflicted cruel deaths upon both of them in the dungeons of the castle of Ferrara.

Consider and discuss all the ways in which people may be imprisoned, entombed or trapped, including historical characters such as Richard I, Elizabeth I, Guy Fawkes, Essex, etc, or in more recent times, prisoners of war, men trapped in mine shafts, people trapped in earthquakes, etc; and the way this is sometimes portrayed in literature, eg

E. A. Poe "The Pit and the Pendulum"
Dumas *The Count of Monte Cristo*
Dickens *A Tale of Two Cities* (chap. vi)
George Orwell *Nineteen Eighty-Four*
Shakespeare Clarence in *Richard III* (Act I sc.iii), *Richard II* (Act V sc.ii)

SUGGESTIONS FOR WORK

1) Write about someone in a cell, perhaps in the form of a diary concealed somehow. Consider nature and place of confinement, as well as the person imprisoned and his adversaries. Either concentrate on the man's story, his life, what sort of person he is, or alternatively concentrate on a detailed description of the situation. A beginning if your are stuck:

> There are holes worn into the stone where my predecessor every day of his imprisonment for thirty years placed his right hand and his left foot to hoist himself up to the chink of light filtering through the slit they call a window. Each hollow is worn beautifully smooth in the stone, almost lovingly moulded by his hand and foot. On the opposite wall, as the sun moved round he has carved the stations of the cross.[1] A religious man then! And what did he gain from his religion...?
>
> When I was brought here yesterday and discovered what these holes were I was seized with horror and then resolved to avoid them. I would not fall into the trap. And yet, this morning, as the sun arose I put my hand into that same place where his hand had been, my foot into that same rounded hollow...

Continue.

[1]Such holes and carvings can be seen in one of the dungeons in Loches. In another, Count Sforza's cell, the walls and ceiling are covered with his painting, since he was allowed to have paint and charcoal.

2) Man or woman in straight jacket. Not mad. Other explanation?
3) Story of miner, potholer or victim of earthquake trapped underground. (Child, old person, young man or woman?)
4) A prisoner in a high tower. From the window of his cell he can see into the street below: passers-by going about their business, women shopping, children playing, etc. Build up a story around this. Is the story set in distant past, in last war, or is it perhaps taking place at some different level of existence? See next item.
5) Write about a prisoner in a room, cell, etc, which leaves us in doubt whether the person is actually imprisoned or whether it is in his mind that he is imprisoned. ("Stone walls do not a prison make, nor iron bars a cage", etc. Use this as title?)
6) Old man, woman, or a child confined to bed. A kind of imprisonment. What can they see? What do they think? (See opening of Beckett's *Malone Dies.)*
7) Alone in a house with all the food necessary, etc. Explanation? Could be a SF story, somebody under house-arrest, psychological story, etc.
8) The question of escape. Having got their hero securely locked away, students might like to devise ways of getting him out. I'll leave that to your own ingenuity!
9) On the other hand, you may be less concerned with the mechanics of the actual escape than with the description of some particular escape. For example, the Earl of Nithsdale, a Scottish nobleman imprisoned in the Jacobite uprisings of 1715, escaped from the Tower disguised as a woman, with the assistance of his wife. You may have to dress up the details, describe the place, the atmosphere, the sense of being in the dungeon, the warders, the stench, the damp, nail-studded doors, etc. You may wish to concentrate on the detail, especially if you have been intrigued by an account of some particular place, by a picture in a book, or by some fortress or dungeon you have visited.
10) Students who have already worked at the section on Interrogation might like to consider a story involving the three elements—Interrogation, Incarceration, Escape.

RESEARCH FOR THOSE INTERESTED

Do a study of the escapes from some fortress, or make a collection of the different kinds of escapes attempted.

WRITING A NOVEL

Probably everyone has a novel in them, and no doubt a lot of publishers wish it would stay that way. Nevertheless, attempting a novel is a challenge many students find it exciting to take up, and certainly for those studying Literature it's a very good way of discovering something of the structure and nature of the form.

It's best to start writing about what you know. "Exotic" experience isn't essential; it's the truth of the experience that's important. You don't have to have lived with the Xingu Indians in Brazil, or have eluded the KGB in Petropavlovsk to create a credible, even illuminating picture of the human condition, though, of course, it might help to broaden your horizons. A man telling you how he almost drowned in the Severn when he was a boy thirty years ago can be as exciting, moving, intriguing as a man telling you how he fell into the Nile, though the crocodiles might *prima facie* look the more thrilling bet than the violence of the currents just below Bridgenorth. This leads me to a point about encouraging children to write.

One of the things you have to do with children in the classroom is convince them that their experience is valuable. It might be watching Dad make something (like Paul watching his father make fuses in *Sons and Lovers,* Chapter IV); overhearing a family row (like Stephen in *A Portrait of the Artist as a Young Man,* Chapter I); playing with water (*Cider with Rosie,* see p 35 this book); losing something (the lost pound note in Raymond Williams' *Border Country,* Chapter IV, Sect. 3); acting as a go-between *(The Go-Between,* L. P. Hartley); watching some creature (the land turtle in *The Grapes of Wrath,* Chapter III); or feeling gauche (the Freak in Carson McCuller's *The Member of the Wedding,* Part I, see p 163 this book). It might be climbing a tree, getting lost, being alone in a house, a death in the family, a broken promise, a memorable visit, flying a kite, stealing, being beaten, running away, etc, etc.

Probably it's easiest to start with an episodic novel, suggested perhaps by the kind of experiences noted above. Collect together a number of memorable or significant experiences. Simply string them together chronologically, or if you like to do something different:

arrange them in flashback, or
look back and forward from some vantage point, or
arrange the experiences in the form of a diary which is incomplete and on which you have to elaborate (see Hartley's *The Go-Between),* or
arrange them in connection with some individual, an aunt, perhaps, or a friend, or
arrange them however you like.

Consider the narrative style. One of the dangers of using the "third-person intimate = I" technique, is that it can become self-indulgent. Sometimes the first person can avoid this, because you are less likely to let yourself become mawkish, for example, using "I". The problem is that as well as becoming self-indulgent, it can become self-enclosed. But it's a matter of taste and personality. Experiment. Try different techniques. Try to be completely objective, try the omnipotent viewpoint. Perhaps alternate, as Dickens does in *Bleak House.* Or try a mixture of third person and interior monologue. By doing this you'll learn far more about the technique of fiction than any amount of lecturing can teach you.

SOME IDEAS FOR WORK

1) Father and mother have a row. Father goes out and gets drunk, mother goes upstairs to pack case. She pauses to look through things, eg blouse bought long ago, photo, a bracelet, etc. Relate the story first as seen through eyes of sensitive child:
   a) In first person looking back,
   b) In third person at the time,
   c) As related years later to the narrator;

then through the eyes of the father as above; then through the eyes of the mother as above. Any other possibilities?
What are they arguing about?

She complains that he doesn't understand her need for some kind of separate imaginative life of her own.

He complains that she doesn't understand the pressure of his work.

Or they both have mild affairs and each complains that the other's affair is more important than they say it is.

Or it's about money.

Or she is stuck in all day with the kid, he is out of a job and each is wounding the other.

Or she is twenty-five and he is fifty-five, or the other way about.

Or one or other is a step-parent.

Or they are arguing about the child, or the baby, or the flat, or his aspirations to be a champion snooker-player or her aspirations to be a poet, etc.

2) Take some experience of your own and examine it from different angles, eg a misunderstanding with a boy/girl friend.
3) Another extension of this work is to take some simple incident (eg an argument at a party, loss of an object, sudden departure, etc. Perhaps child is accused of responsibility) and systematically, relate it as seen through eyes of all of the group, leaving the child until the last.
4) Something-nasty-in-the-woodshed idea. (See Graham Greene's "The Potting Shed".) Some experience from which you, or your protagonist, has been cut off, ie a crucial explanation or fact is lacking and haunts you over the years. Detective work to find out what it is. How? Diary, letters, chance conversation, meeting, etc. What sort of experience?
5) But most people want to write a straight-forward chronological narrative, either dealing with their own life from childhood to the present into maturity (the *Bildungsroman* as it's called), or an account of a period of a few days, or weeks, one summer holiday, say, or a trip abroad, working in a café, shop, factory, etc.
6) Some people find it difficult just to start—remember you can always change it later. Here are some simple possible openings:

> She lay staring up at the ceiling. Another day of predictable events. She would wash, dress, eat, catch the eight-thirty, arrive at the shop a minute late, say good morning to the teaboy, to Mr Williams. To what purpose?
>
> For a long time she followed the crack in the plaster to the edges where the moulding met the walls. Eventually, even that pattern of journeys became predictable...

> We were jogging along in the waggon somewhere out in the country and I remembered that other time...

> In those days there were trees behind the houses and from the bedroom you could see the meadow, the hills beyond, the gasworks, and the black church standing like an elongated bat with its ears erect...

> The office door opened and a tall thin man carrying a violin-case and wearing a long black overcoat entered...

7) Of course, some people find it more manageable to make the setting for their adventures somewhere remote or imagined; for example, you can be bored, or find life predictable in a hotel room in Calcutta, or in a flat in Rio de Janiero, just as you can in Muswell Hill or Manchester.
8) But if you are trying to get children to write novels you will need eventually to give them scope, some fantasy, some adventure, something *new.* See Ted Hughes' four openings in "Writing a Novel".[1] Suggest that children write a short chapter, say a page or two pages a day, which is about manageable, or they can do some at odd times when they like. Some possible openings:

   SCIENCE FICTION

   He woke suddenly. The whole house was shaking...

   ADVENTURE

   The sun was pounding the sand and each step was harder than the last. He looked back but could no longer see the smoking aircraft...

   FANTASY OR REALITY

   She opened the window and looked out. Her mother was talking to the housekeeper. The house seemed huge to Susan. There was so much to explore...

---

[1]In *Poetry in the Making* (Faber)

INNOVATION

This section is concerned with the nature of expression and the need to explore new forms of representing our apprehension of the world.

According to Susanne Langer[1] we need art because only through art can we express what is inexpressible in terms of other modes of thinking—Science, Mathematics, Politics, etc. She puts it like this in a lecture on the cultural importance of art:

> Art (i.e. music, dance, literature, drama, films, etc) may be defined as the practice of creating perceptible forms expressive of human feeling...[2]

She goes on to explain what she means by "forms", "expressive", and "feeling", pointing out that she does not limit her concept to the meaning in such expressions as, say, a "tender feeling", or "harrowing" one's feelings. She is thinking of whatever is within us that forms our INNER LIFE, which is not necessarily amenable to expression in ratiocinative terms; or, to put it in the vernacular, whatever can't easily be got into the ordinary sequential forms of argument, logic, and thought patterning, that philosophy, science, etc, offer us. One sometimes sees a painting, for example, and feels that the painting has expressed subtly what it might have taken volumes of words to point at only very crudely; or in reading a poem one may respond to some elusive idea that exists in the interstices of language, in the spaces between the words, as an electrical spark may exist between two poles when a current is discharged through it. D. H. Lawrence has a little poem called, significantly, "Terra Incognita" (unknown land) in which he attempts to chart these inaccessible regions of our minds, and perhaps, in some senses, succeeds in saying something illuminating about the "unsayable":

---

[1] *Philosophy in a New Key* (Signet Books)

[2] From "The Cultural Importance of Art" in *Philosophical Sketches* (Signet Books)

There are vast realms of consciousness still undreamed of
vast ranges of experience, like the humming of
unseen harps,
we know nothing of, within us.

Oh when man escapes from the barbed-wire entanglement
of his own ideas and his own mechanical devices
there is a marvellous rich world of contact and sheer
fluid beauty
and fearless face-to-face awareness of now-naked life
and me, and you, and other men and women
and grapes, and ghouls, and ghosts and green moonlight
and ruddy-orange limbs stirring the limbo
of the unknown air, and eyes so soft
softer than the space between the stars,
and all things, and nothing, and being and not-being
alternately palpitant;
when at last we escape the barbed-wire enclosure
of Know Thyself, *knowing we can never know,*
we can but touch, and wonder, and ponder, and make
our effort
and dangle in a last fastidious fine delight
as the fuschia does, dangling her reckless drop
of purple after so much putting forth
and slow mounting marvel of a little tree.[1]

Perhaps most of human culture, most civilization has been concerned with finding ways of expressing this *inner life,* what Miss Langer, for want of a better term, calls "feeling". We do it when we talk to each other, when we paint or respond to a piece of music, perhaps even when we ponder on psycho-analytical accounts of human behaviour. Much of this is arguable, or contentious, and perhaps students will find it interesting to discuss it, possibly in conjunction with Susanne Langer's essay. The point I want to take up here specifically is the question of FORM, the way of putting that inner life into some kind of shape.

We try to find a form which will best express what we want to say: Please Keep off the Grass, Keep off the Grass, People who walk on the grass are rotten Swine, etc; or "Love is not love which alters where it alteration finds", or "I sang in my chains like the sea". To

[1] *Colletcted Poems* (Heinemann)

put it more succinctly, we look for a form which will re-create in words "what oft was thought but ne'er so well expressed", to borrow Pope's definition of Wit. We have an idea, a feeling, an attitude, a kind of elusive awareness of something and we need to organize it in some way. Here is Ted Hughes commenting on this relationship between language and thought:

> There is the inner life, which is the world of final reality, the world of memory, emotion, imagination, intelligence, and natural commonsense, and which goes on all the time, consciously or unconsciously, like the heartbeat. There is also the thinking process by which we break into that inner life and capture answers and evidence to support the answers out of it. That process of raid, or persuasion, or ambush, or dogged hunting, or surrender, is the kind of thinking we have to learn and if we do not somehow learn it, then our minds lie in us like the fish in the pond of a man who cannot fish.[1]

But more often than not the tackle, the materials at our disposal (let's keep to language for the sake of simplicity), the *words* we have to use and the forms conventionally accepted for using them in seem inadequate. Incidentally, it is worth remembering that, for example, putting thoughts into sentences with ideas following sequentially (rather than perhaps simultaneously) is only a convention we have adopted (putting ideas in lines, writing from left to right, etc). Consider the Chinese idiographs, Egyptian hieroglyphs. At any rate it is interesting to consider the implications of the above—that the notion of "correct" forms derives only from conventionally accepted disciplines. The point I am making is that the notion of what is correct may be restrictive, and that the artist may need to challenge it, or alter it, or he may feel that he will simply have to avoid it. Hence INNOVATION.

The writer attempting to say something about the anxiety of modern life may feel that one single word on an otherwise empty page may have more impact than a closely reasoned critique:

---

[1]From *Poetry in the Making* (Faber)

HELP!

José Paulo Paes used a similar approach in his modification of Descartes's famous "cogito ergo sum" conclusion. You'll remember that Descartes set himself to doubt everything that could be doubted and came to the conclusion that the only thing that was indubitable was that he was doubting, hence: "I think, therefore I am". Edwin Morgan translated the little piece as follows:

The Suicide, or Descartes à Rebours[1]

cogito

ergo

boom

You may argue about the implications of that. Perhaps the space between the words represents the universe, perhaps the words suggest an ironic view of man's achievement, perhaps it represents a failure in communication.

The point is that the way a thing is expressed depends on the idea and the originator of the idea, and his need to express it in a way he thinks appropriate. We shouldn't therefore be too anxious to repudiate or dismiss a form because it fails to accord with our ideas of the conventional modes of expression. The writer is in a constant dilemma between the notions in his head or in his nervous system (and perhaps it is permissible to talk of such a thing—see D. W. Harding's *Experience into Words*[2]) and the means he has to express these notions. As T. S. Eliot says in "Burnt Norton":

---

[1]*Times Literary Supplement,* September 3 1964 [2]Chatto & Windus/Peregrine

Words strain,
Crack and sometimes break, under the burden,
Under the tension slip, slide, perish,
Decay with imprecision, will not stay in place,
Will not stay still.[1]

As soon as the writer gets his words down, he is confronted with the problem that they do not really convey what is in his head, or "inner life"; the words seem unstable, they won't hold the thought as a goblet might hold wine. Every time a writer thinks he has learned a trick that will hold the idea still long enough for him to look at it, he discovers that it is a trick or technique for what he doesn't want to say any more—he has moved on:

And so each venture
Is a new beginning, a raid on the inarticulate
With shabby equipment always deteriorating
In the general mess of imprecision of feeling,
Undisciplined squads of emotion...[2]

The Chinese poet Lu Chi wrestles with the same problem.
He puts it like this:

We poets struggle with Non-being to force it
to yield being:
We knock upon silence for an answering music.
We enclose boundless space in a square foot of paper:
We pour out deluge from the inch of space of the heart.[3]

We could spend a lot more time on the problems, but perhaps enough has been said to indicate the nature of the choice facing the creative artist and to indicate reasons why he might not choose a conventional pattern. The history of English Literature is a story of constant change, continual innovative processes, from Wyatt's adaption of the Italian sonnet to Joyce's exploitation of the language's ambiguity and mythical potential:

---

[1]"Burnt Norton" V in *Four Quartets* (Faber)
[2]T. S. Eliot "East Coker" V in *Four Quartets* (Faber)
[3]Translation by Achilles Fang first published in *New Mexico Quarterly.* Quoted by Archibald McLeish in *Poetry & Experience* (Bodley Head)

> Sir Tristram, violer d'amores, fr'over the short sea, had passencore rearrived from North Amorica on this side the scraggy isthmus of Europe Minor to wielderfight his penisolate war.[1]

It seems to be the case that no sooner is a form acceptable than it becomes a "norm", and when this happens it is of course questioned or challenged. As early as the eighteenth century Sterne was making fun of the Novel.[2] The novel was then only just established. In *The Common Reader* Virginia Woolf draws attention to the compulsion on the novelist to conform (see p 59). She claims that the writer shouldn't be easily seduced into a mode which may not be the most suitable way for him to examine the nature of truth, which is after all what art is about. Joyce attempted early on in *Ulysses*[3] to tackle the problem of the inner life. Here is an extract in which Mr Bloom is walking to the butcher's shop early in the morning to buy some kidneys for his breakfast. We move from what he can see and appreciate with his senses to what is going on more or less unformed, inchoately in his head. I say "more or less", because even in free association we see some connections between one idea and another, however diverse they may appear. Also, of course, Joyce cannot show the totality in the mind of a man, he has to select, to offer samples, so to speak; we judge his achievement on the skill with which he has been selective:

> He crossed to the bright side, avoiding the loose cellarflap of number seventyfive. The sun was nearing the steeple of George's church. Be a warm day I fancy. Specially in these black clothes feel it more. Black conducts, reflects (refracts is it?), the heat. But I couldn't go in that light suit. Make a picnic of it. His eyelids sank quietly often as he walked in happy warmth. Boland's breadvan delivering with trays our daily but she prefers yesterday's loaves turnovers crisp crowns hot. Makes you feel young. Somewhere in the east: early morning: set off at dawn, travel round in front of the sun, steal a day's march on him. Keep it up for ever never grow a day older technically. Walk along a strand, strange land, come to a city gate, sentry there, old ranker too, old Tweedy's big moustaches leaning on a long kind of spear. Wander through awned streets. Turbaned faces going by. Dark caves of carpet shops, big man, Turko the terrible, seated crosslegged smoking a coiled pipe. Cries of sellers in the streets. Drink water scented

---

[1] *Finnegans Wake* (Faber) [2] *Tristram Shandy* [3] Bodley Head/Penguin

> with fennel, sherbet. Wander along all day. Might meet a robber or two. Well, meet him. Getting on to sundown. The shadows of the mosques along the pillars: priest with a scroll rolled up. A shiver of the trees, signal, the evening wind. I pass on. Fading gold sky. A mother watches from her doorway. She calls her children home in their dark language. High wall: beyond strings twanged. Night sky moon, violet, colour of Molly's new garters. Strings. Listen. A girl playing one of these instruments what do you call them: dulcimers. I pass.

We see here how Mr Bloom's thoughts move from the light and warmth of the sun to the black clothes he is wearing in order to attend a funeral later in the day; how the warmth and the new bread make him feel young again, and how ideas of the sun's movement, rising in the east, relating to time and youth, coalesce with his own mental image of the East, mixed as it is with his father-in-law (old Tweedy, a professional soldier in Gibralter) and a pantomime character his mother used to admire, called Turko the terrible; how his images of the colours and the exotic richness of his vision of the place is connected with his opulent Molly; and how his reading has half thrown up the "girl with a dulcimer" *(A damsel with a dulcimer/In a vision once I saw/It was an Abyssinian maid/And on her dulcimer she played)*[1] – which is perhaps the author himself giving us a hint about how the process works.

And, of course, there have been many subsequent attempts to probe the nature of the novel's form in the process of writing something for which only the form of the novel seems suitable. B. S. Johnson once wrote a novel which he offered in separable sections and boxed so that the reader could read it in random fashion and reconstruct it as he liked. In another novel, *Albert Angelo,*[2] Johnson has in one part of the book two-column pages: on the left is the scene in the classroom as it is happening, on the right are represented the narrator's thoughts taking place simultaneously. Johnson is trying to find new ways of indicating the inner and outer life. Here is an extract from the book:

---

[1]Coleridge *Kubla Khan* [2]Constable/Panther

— —No, but I will do.

Stupid truculence. Have to hit him now.

All right, little one, come out here. You did hear me say 'no talking', didn't you?

Eyes narrowly, skin very white, hands just like trotters and dirty, nicotine-stained.

I asked you a question! Did you hear me say 'no talking'?
— —No, but I w… oh! You ent sposed to 'it kids on the 'ead!

All violence rebounds on society. He'll take it out on another kid. Or on something.

Just go and sit down and don't let me hear another word from you unless I ask for it. And what's your name? What's your name!

But what hurt did I just now pass on? It must stop somewhere, but why with me? Or is there a constant quantity of violence in the world, continually circulating?

— —Langley.
Langley.
— —'E'll 'ave to go, then, them suedes 'n' all, the lot!

Right, settle down, I know it's the last lesson of the day and you can't wait to get home, but first you're going to listen very carefully to a Geology lesson. What's Geology? Langley? Anyone else?

Nor can I, for that matter.

— —It's to do with dirt and stones and stuff like that.

Yes, that's nearly right. Geology is the study of earth and stones and everything that goes to make up the world except for the living things like plants and animals. And ourselves. Have you learnt anything about this subject before?
— —No.
— —No.

— — Don't want to know.
— — No.
Not in Geography lessons?
Nothing at all?

Thick. Or resentful. And. Can't get any response today. Either. Haven't tried very hard. Guilt. But tiredness. C-stream, too, christ knows what the H-stream must be like!

Then I'll have to start right from the beginning. You all know what stone is, and that there are different

Even that assuming too much? Cynical, cynical.

Students might like to consider this. How often is one abstracted from the surrounding conversation, the inner self ticking over in its own fashion like an engine idling, while all around is activity of some kind. Try writing a sequence where there is conversation going on all round, at a party, for example, or in a coffee bar, while the mind of the individual wanders in free association, or in connection with what is being said, as fragments of the pervasive conversation impinge.

And here are some more examples students might like to discuss or use as a basis for their own experiments:

1) Miss Kennedy sauntered sadly from bright light, twining a loose hair behind an ear. Sauntering sadly, gold no more, she twisted twined a hair. Sadly she twined in sauntering gold hair behind a curving ear.

Yes, bronze from anear, by gold from afar, heard steel from anear, hoofs ring from afar, and heard steelhoofs ringhoof ringsteel.

Her wavyavyeavyheavyeavyevyevy hair un comb: 'd

The extracts here come from the Sirens episode in *Ulysses*.[1] The prevailing mode and indeed the structure of this section is music. There are dozens of musical references and allusions, but Joyce also uses words as though they were notes or phrases in music, repeating, breaking them up, alternating them *(her wavyavyeavyheavyeavyevyevy hair un comb: 'd* for instance is a kind of trill with an Italian turn at the end).

[1]Bodley Head/Penguin

2) *Earnest, earthless, equal, attuneable,   vaulty, voluminous,... stupendous*
Evening strains to be tíme's vást,   womb-of-all, home-of-all, hearse-of-all night.
Her fond yellow hornlight wound to the west,   her wild hollow hoarlight hung to the height
Waste; her earliest stars, earl-stars,   stárs principal, overbend us,
Fíre-féaturing heaven. For earth   her being has unbound, her dapple is at an end, as–
tray or aswarm, all throughther, in throngs; self ín self steepèd and páshed – qúite
Disremembering, dísmémbering áll now.

This is from a poem by Gerard Manley Hopkins titled "Spelt from Sibyl's Leaves" and is, in fact, the first seven lines of a sonnet. Discuss the effects Hopkins creates in setting out his poem in this way.

3) *Twit twit twit*
Jug jug jug jug jug jug
So rudely forc'd.
Tereu
Unreal City
Under the brown fog of a winter noon
Mr Eugenides, the Smyrna merchant
Unshaven, with a pocket full of currants
C.i.f. London: documents at sight
Asked me in demotic French
To luncheon at the Cannon Street Hotel
Followed by a weekend at the Metropole.

An extract from "The Waste Land" by T. S. Eliot.[1] In this section several elements (single words or phrases) are brought together from diverse parts of the poem and overlaid, so to speak, as they might be in music. If you're familiar with Wagner's *Ring of the Nibelung* then you'll understand the way the composer uses *leitmotif.* Here Eliot is doing something similar. Use any of these ideas to experiment in your own writing.

[1]In *The Waste Land and Other Poems* (Faber)

4) FOLDED POEM

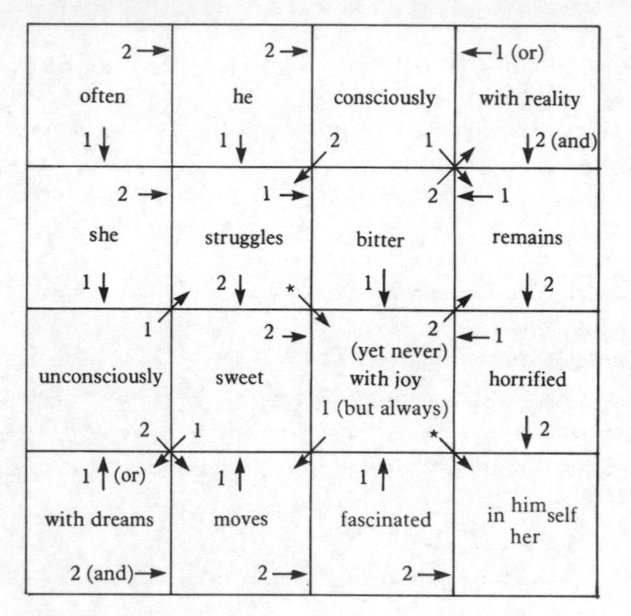

Instructions:

1. Begin at the "often" square.
2. Toss a coin: head=1, tail=2.
3. Move according to arrow (e.g.: in first square if you've a head, move to "she", if a tail to "he").
4. In "struggles" and "with joy" squares throw two coins, if they show the same, follow the * arrow; if not toss a single coin again as usual.
5. Add words bracketed by arrows in some squares, after the word in the square.
6. Add words of your own if you dislike solecisms; cheat if you dislike repetition; give up if you're looking for a logical or reasoned pattern. Profundity is in the eye of the beholder.[1]

This is by Mark Holloway who when he wrote it was a pupil at St Paul's School, London. Work through it. Discuss the implications of it. Try one of your own.

For other work connected with Innovation see next section on Concrete Poetry.

---

[1]In *Workshop 20* (Workshop Press)

CONCRETE POETRY

Several references have been made already to concrete poetry and for the benefit of those students to whom the term is unfamiliar, perhaps it is as well to say something about it. It seems to have originated independently in Brazil and Germany as a way of describing forms of verbal expression which depend less on the conventional structures of syntax and sentence formation than on the visual and semantic effect of words or word elements, sometimes used independently and sometimes arranged in typographical patterns. The *cogito ergo boom* piece given on p 127 is an example. Here are some more[1]:

```
        STAR
       STAR
      STAR
     star
    STAR
     STAR
      STAR
       STAR
        STAR
       STAR
      STAR
     STAR
    steer
```

Dogs Round a Tree

```
             ow!
            wow!
        bowwow!
       !bowwow!
      w!bowwo
     ow!boww
    wow!bow
   wwow!bo
  owwow!b
 bowwow!
    wow!
     ow!
```

[1]"Star" and "Silence" by Ian Hamilton Finlay and Eugene Goningen in *Concrete Poetry* (Indiana Press) and *Times Literary Supplement* September 3 1964; "Dogs Round a Tree", "T Poem" and "Opening the Cage" by Edwin Morgan in *The Second Life* (Edinburgh University Press)

Silence silence silence
silence silence silence
silence silence
silence silence silence
silence silence silence

T Poem

Parties, Pots, Cozys
Trays, Time, Caddies
Kettles, Roses, Cups
Tables
Leaves
Cloths
Houses
Spoons
Shirts
Chests
Things

OPENING THE CAGE: 14 variations on 14 words
I have nothing to say and I am saying it and that is poetry.
John Cage.

I have to say poetry and is that nothing and am I saying it
I am and I have poetry to say and is that nothing saying it
I am nothing and I have poetry to say and that is saying it
I that am saying poetry have nothing and it is I and to say
And I say that I am to have poetry and saying it is nothing
I am poetry and nothing and saying it is to say that I have
To have nothing is poetry and I am saying that and I say it
Poetry is saying I have nothing and I am to say that and it
Saying nothing I am poetry and I have to say that and it is
It is and I am and I have poetry saying say that to nothing
It is saying poetry to nothing and I say I have and am that
Poetry is saying I have it and I am nothing and to say that
And that nothing is poetry I am saying and I have to say it
Saying poetry is nothing and to that I say I am and have it

Edwin Morgan

Perhaps students might like to try some, typing them out (the typewriter will produce its own quite automatically if you're not careful!), or drawing them, or making them in the form of posters. It's best just to experiment, but if you find difficulty, try one along the lines of Edwin Morgan's "T Poem", say, on WHEELS, FLOWERS, MONEY, or what ever occurs to you.

Take a word or phrase and arrange it, play with it, take it for a walk. (Paul Klee said that drawing was taking a line for a walk. Perhaps you can do the same with a word.)

Here's a simple one with FOG:

o

F

g

og

F

g

o

and another with BUTTERFLY:

FLUTTER

BYUTTERLY

FLUTE

FLY BERTLY

LUTEFUL

FL

T

BUT

FLUTEBLE

Try some concrete poems on Wind Sounds or Sea Sounds or Sky Shapes. See Apollinaire's poem "It's Raining" in Appendix p 173.)

Take a word such as GOLD. What images does it evoke in your mind? Jot them down and then try to arrange or disjoint them so that they make some kind of typographical pattern, perhaps in the shape of the theme.

Remember: you can make a list, write a poem, put the words anywhere on the paper, put them into a pattern, colour them, use letters or type of different sizes, fold the paper, cut it up, paste words on, look in the Dictionary for source and play with roots, and different meanings of words.

And what's the point of it all? One answer might be that it's an opportunity to exercise your ingenuity. Discuss any other reasons why you think writers might be interested in this form of expression.

MYTH

A subject so vast, so rich in material, ideas, images, stories, that the prospecting writer can plunder anywhere and find gold: from the challenge of these glimpses of man's earliest attempts to come to terms with his fears and aspirations or to understand the nature of the universe by thinking allegorically or symbolically, to the single images, fragments of the stories that linger in the imagination and fecundate it. Think, for instance, of the moment when Orpheus looks back on Eurydice on their journey out of the Underworld, thus losing her forever; or of the moment when Midas touches the rose, or, in one version, his daughter; or of the drops of blood from the wound of Hyacinthus which Apollo caused to be transformed into flowers. Or consider the rich poetic implications in the stories of Pandora and her box of evils which she released on mankind, leaving only Hope behind (see George Herbert's poem "The Pulley" which uses the story but in a contrary way); or the cult of Adonis whose body is interred like Persephone's for half of the year to rise again in the growing crops and vines (see J. G. Frazer's classical anthropological work *The Golden Bough*[1] and Eliot's "The Waste Land").

There are many ways in which students might draw on Myth, and one useful thing to do would be to consider a few of the myths and discuss how they might be employed, or have been employed. Take

[1]The Macmillan Press

the story of Clyte and the Sun God Hyperion, for instance, in which Clyte gazing at the Sun all day, rejected by him, becomes rooted to the earth and follows his course through the heavens. Compare this with Blake's short poem "Ah, Sun-Flower":

Ah, sun-flower! weary of time,
Who countest the steps of the sun,
Seeking after that sweet golden clime
Where the traveller's journey is done;

Where the youth pined away with desire,
And the pale virgin shrouded in snow,
Arise from their graves, and aspire
Where my sun-flower wishes to go.

Or consider the account of Zeus's visit to the beautiful Leda in the form of a swan (an encounter which led to the birth of Helen of Troy), which Yeats represents in his "Leda and the Swan"[1];

A sudden blow: the great wings beating still
Above the staggering girl, her thighs caressed
By the dark webs, her nape caught in his bill,
He holds her helpless breast upon his breast.

How can those terrified vague fingers push
The feathered glory from her loosening thighs?
And how can body, laid in that white rush,
But feel the strange heart beating where it lies?

A shudder in the loins engenders there
The broken wall, the burning roof and tower
And Agamemnon dead.
Being so caught up,
So mastered by the brute blood of the air,
Did she put on his knowledge with his power
Before the indifferent beak could let her drop?

Which some consider as representing the rape of mankind by divinity, and others the infusion of creative energy into humanity.

Or take the story of Aurora and Tithonus (see p 109). In Tennyson's poem "Tithonus" he bemoans his condition compared with other creatures: "after many a summer dies the swan". See also Tennyson's treatment of Ulysses, Oenone, and The Lotus Eaters;

---

[1]In *Collected Poems* (Macmillan)

D. H. Lawrence's "Bavarian Gentians"; Shakespeare's "Phoenix and the Turtle"; Elizabeth Barrett Browning's "A Musical Instrument".

Students might like to take some moment from one of the myths which they find particularly appealing, and treat it in a short poem. Some suggestions:

Flight of Icarus
Phaeton's journey through the sky in the chariot of the Sun
Battle between Bellerophon, riding the winged horse Pegasus, and the Chimera
The fall of Hephaestus (cf. Milton in *Paradise Lost* Bk I[1])
Prometheus stealing fire from the Gods
Prometheus on the rock
Andromeda chained to the rock
Glaucus under the sea (cf. Keats' version in "Endymion" Book III)
Orpheus looking back on Eurydice (cf. Anouilh's treatment of the story in *Point of Departure)*

Another approach is to consider some of the stories and their use to inform modern stories or plays, eg: E. M. Forster's use of the apotheosis of Oedipus at Colonus in his short story "The Road from Colonus" (cf. with Sophocles in the second Thebean play), Ben Hecht's basing of his play *The Rape of the Belt* on Heracles' visit to the land of the Amazon women. Students might do two things here. One is to take the basic outline of a myth (eg Glaucus and Scylla, Pandora, Midas, Pygmalion and Galatea, etc) and write it as a story, filling out the detail (Pandora's growing curiosity, Glaucus under the sea, etc). As a piece for discussion students might consider the opening of Garfield and Blishen's *The God Beneath the Sea*[2]:

> At first it was a tiny prick of light—as if the sun had gone too close and caught the immense blue fabric of the sky. It glinted and glittered and presently it was seen to be moving, like a golden needle stitching away at the heavens.
>
> This was in the early morning. By noon its brightness had dimmed. Against the sun's full blaze it was no more than a charred

[1]Milton uses the image of Hephaestus' fall to enhance his account of Satan's fall:

> *From morn*
> *To noon he fell, from noon to dewy eve,*
> *A summer's day, and with the setting sun*
> *Dropped from the zenith, like a falling star,*
> *On Lemnos, the Aegean isle.*

[2]Longman/Corgi

and flaming mote. The sun continued toward the west; the sky deepened and the mote had increased till it was the size of a thumbnail held at full stretch.

Already its light cast a great pool of gold on the darkening sea and a curious sound was in the air. A thin wailing that rose at times to a scream...

Now the sun was gone and the twisting, flickering, shining thing lit up a patch of the night as it rushed down to meet itself in the sea.

The sound grew shriller, louder. The waves began to tremble and hasten hither and thither in a panic. It was coming....Then, for the briefest instant, the falling shape was seen quite clearly as it turned over and over in the air. It was a fiery, shrieking baby...

Suddenly two white arms rose up out of the sea. They caught the infant as it fell and drew it swiftly down under the wave. The light was quenched and the sea rolled on, dark and peaceful under the stars.

The gaping fish and the blundering turtles fled away; the ornamental sea-horses and giant crabs that seemed to carry spired and blushing cities on their backs drifted and clambered into nooks and crevices as the goddess sped down among them in a pearly storm of bubbles.

Deeper and deeper she rushed with the frantic infant in her arms. The formidable monsters on the ocean's floor curled and rolled away among the coral forests where the flash and glimmer of sea-nymphs lit the goddess on her way. At last she came to the entrance of a cave. Here, strange and intricate configurations of the rock caused the currents to twist and eddy and force the waters through a mighty conch shell so that they foamed and tumbled across the cave's threshold like the fleece of the sea-god's sheep.

The goddess paused, then stepped across the waters into the cave and the grotto beyond.

Perhaps students might think of their version as one to use with children in order to encourage them to paint, write poetry, or perhaps make a sound play on tape.

Alternatively students might be attracted to the idea of using one of the myths as the basis for a modern story dressing it up with contemporary trappings in a contemporary situation—Midas overwhelmed with desire for gold gets his wish and everything he touches turns to gold, including all living things. How might this be treated?

A man ruthlessly pursuing his ambition to become wealthy, destroying relationships in the process...

Obviously, the stories could be retold as modern horror stories, using all the violence and blood-letting of the originals (Philomel and Tereus, Oedipus, Agamemnon). They might also, of course, be transformed, so that a murder is replaced with, say, a character assassination, a destruction of personality or power, sexual defeat, etc. In other words, the axe that falls on Agamemnon in the bath might be a different kind of axe, a verbal blow, a crushing discovery. Similarly, the search for Eurydice might be a search for poetry, beauty, truth, lost imagination, in the way that the shepherd Endymion's enchantment by the moon is depicted by Keats as a kind of enthralment by poetry and the world of the imagination. It is more than likely that many of the great, complex and violent myths (such as the story of Oedipus, Agamemnon, Zeus's castration of his father Chronos, etc) are allegorical renderings of ideas or fears or anxieties.[1] Students might think of what lies behind such myths and of ways of conveying the same story in modern terms. The monster in the Labyrinth might be jealousy, or guilt, or fear; the head of Medusa, anything too horrible to contemplate; or the fine golden nets which Hephaestus forged with gold thread so delicate it was imperceptible and in which he enmeshed his wife Venus and Mars her lover, might be any kind of subtle trick.

FOR REFERENCE SEE

Robert Graves *The Greek Myths* (Pelican)
Thomas Bulfinch *The Age of Fable* (Mentor)

[1]See Brown *Freud and the Post Freudians* (Pelican)

FREUD AND THE FAIRY TALE

"Freudian" elements in Myth and Fairy Tale are probably familiar to anyone who is adult and has grown up with, and continued to enjoy, these stories. The throwing-off of parental control, the overthrowing of the old regime, is clearly evident in the myth of Chronos, where Zeus castrates his father and usurps his power over the gods; as is the adolescent awakening of the girl into maturity in the perennial favourite Sleeping Beauty. Little Red Riding Hood, leaving the parental protection, is lured by the wolf in the forest, courts danger by giving him specific directions to her grandmother's house and instructions how to get in, faces the threat of being devoured, and narrowly escapes brutal seduction by the sudden appearance of the protective father. (In some versions she is actually devoured by the wolf.) Bruno Bettelheim in an illuminating and delightfully readable account of the psychological patterns in Fairy Tale[1] makes the point that children growing up with fairy tales take from them whatever they need, responding to them according to their stage of development. Consequently, the less explicit or less precisely delineated the basic problem in the story, the wider the relevance. Perrault, he notes, in his account of the Little Red Riding Hood story, belabours the moral—Red Riding Hood straying from the path of virtue, etc.

Consider some of the elements and recurring patterns in fairy tales: breaking out of parental control, or, to see it another way, losing parental protection; setting out on a journey; the youngest (and least regarded) of three brothers, or the poor girl or boy, making good; beauty and the beast; threat from the powers of evil in the form of a wizard or witch; being trapped and escaping, etc. What others occur to you? Discuss them.

SUGGESTIONS FOR WORK

1) Write a story incorporating whatever elements you find interesting from Fairy Tale.

---

[1] *The Uses of Enchantment* (Thames & Hudson)

2) Rewrite or retell a fairy story in modern terms. If you find this difficult, try to plan out a tale using a sequence of three: a soldier sets out on a journey to find his fortune, encounters three people/has three adventures/tackles three tasks/learns three things, etc. The soldier might be a young man who sets out on foot, hitch-hiking, or on a motor-bike, etc.
3) Take one of the stories from folk-lore or legend and arrange it as a sound play for tape, indicating music or sound effects which might be appropriate. Some stories which might be suitable: Legend of Vanderdecken (the Flying Dutchman), Baldur, Emperor's New Clothes, Morgana le Fay, Jack and the Beanstalk/Giantkiller, Lamia (see Keats' poem).
4) Perhaps the simplest (and yet in other ways, most demanding) form of story to write is the quest represented as an allegory or parable. Louis MacNeice[1] in a memorable radio version did this with Browning's "Child Roland to the Dark Tower came", which in its turn had grown out of a line sung by Edgar in *King Lear.* After an arduous journey over difficult terrain the young knight comes to the dark tower and challenges whatever it represents. Think of other quests: *Everyman, Peer Gynt, The Pilgrim's Progress,* Percival in the Arthurian Legend. Students might like to devise their own "quest".

LANDSCAPE OF THE MIND

The mind has its own terrains, mountains, rooms, deserts, streets, battlefields. Try to explore one such landscape of the mind.

Close your eyes and try to visualize a dream landscape—a garden perhaps, or a room, or a desert, or whatever. Remember that in a dream you can be walking on or through anything; things can dissolve, change shape, be transformed; you can walk through mirrors, from a room to a city, into a forest, etc. Let your imagination roam freely. Jot down any images or ideas that occur to you. Imagine that you reach out your hands (remember that tactile element considered in the Hands section p 15) and touch things: stuff, material, glass, ice, wood, etc. Keep walking until... What? You come to a castle/bridge/door/another human being?

[1] Louis MacNeice *The Dark Tower* (Faber)

Is it all in black and white, or colour? What are the shades, shadows, contrasts? Is it all in silent dumb-show, or is there sound, music perhaps?

Begin a story with a single, solitary character sitting in a room. Perhaps the room is empty but for a chair. Is there a door or window? Enter the mind of the character. Explore its landscape.

Compile, write, or make a tape-recording of a sequence of dream landscapes, in which you move through each successively. To what?

Imagine you are in a room of an old house you are visiting or lodging in. You hear voices, vague distant voices, snatches of song, see figures from the past. Think of the room as a palimpsest of all past events enacted in that room, and you are able to move through them.

Suppose the dream landscape is your own, in which are fragments of your experiences, ideas, reading: images of pictures, people, films you have seen, pieces of poems and stories you have read, characters from reality, history, myth, or imagination. Jot down the ideas and then put them into some form, with linking passages perhaps.

CONSIDER OR READ THE FOLLOWING:

T. S. Eliot "The Waste Land"
Ted Hughes "The Wound" in *Wodwo*
Jean-Paul Sartre *Huis Clos* (In Camera)
Franz Kafka *The Castle*
Lewis Carroll *Alice in Wonderland*
William Langland *Piers Ploughman*
John Bunyan *The Pilgrim's Progress*

MUSIC

Debussy "La Cathédrale Engloutie"
Richard Strauss *Death and Transfiguration*
Sibelius "The Bard"
Wagner *Das Rheingold* (Opening)
Haydn *Creation* (Opening)
Ligeti *Atmospheres*
Oldfield *Tubular Bells*

WHAT THE WRITERS SAY

There seems to be as much variety of attitude to and understanding of the creative processes among writers as there is among commentators and critics. This is not the place to examine the relative merits of these differing views in any detail, but it is worthwhile for students to consider the *obiter dicta* of writers and the general areas of interest they examine. If there is any kind of consensus, it is that the writers can't very easily control the processes of creativity, although, of course, they attempt to organize them in various ways for the sake of what might be called "production", and perhaps also for the sake of sanity. The story of the writer staring for hours at a blank page, unable to make a mark on it, or dismantling his typewriter or rearranging his room or, in fact, doing anything rather than bring himself to put words to paper is very common. Some writers comment on the accidental factors involved—the chance connection of two ideas throwing up something completely new; some are interested in the business of an idea or experience nagging away, sometimes for years; some are obsessed with the process of generating images; while for others the nature of observation seems paramount; and most think of their work as a process of exploration—"invent a jungle and then explore it", says the poet Tony Connor.[1] Generally, writers asked to talk about their work comment on the thing that is uppermost in their minds at the moment; and often they tend to regard matters such as the technique of writing a villanelle as matters of craft, that they have learnt or patiently acquired that are not worth comment, or are no business of the reader, just as a shoemaker might not think it relevant or important to describe to you how he has made your shoes, or as a carpenter might offer you a table but is unlikely to present you with a commentary of the difficulties he's had making it.

A process that seems to have interested Dylan Thomas a good deal was the business of generating images, which he seems to have done sometimes with a euphoric gusto that delighted more in the act of creation than in the sense that informed the final draft of the

[1]Quoted in Robin Skelton's *The Practice of Poetry* (Heinemann)

work.[1] I imagine anyone who has only glanced through his poetry will come away with an impression of the richness and variety of his imagery. Particularly in the early poetry, such as the sonnet sequence for instance, he seems fascinated by the craft of working out the implications of his metaphors in terms of other metaphors:

> *Altarwise by owl-light in the half-way house*
> *The gentleman lay graveward with his furies;*
> *Abaddon in the hangnail cracked from Adam,*
> *And, from his fork, a dog among the fairies,*
> *The atlas-eater with the jaw for news,*
> *Bit out the mandrake with tomorrow's scream.*
> *Then, penny-eyed, that gentleman of wounds,*
> *Old cock from nowheres and the heaven's egg,*
> *With bones unbottoned to the half-way winds,*
> *Hatched from the windy salvage on one leg,*
> *Scraped at my cradle in a walking word*
> *That night of time under the Christward shelter:*
> *I am the long world's gentleman, he said,*
> *And share my bed with Capricorn and Cancer.*[2]

Something to do with Christ, Death, Life, The Word, the organ of generation, birth, etc? I've put it like this because the poem certainly isn't ratiocinative, in the way that, shall we say, a sonnet by Shakespeare is—and Shakespeare in his sonnets tends to explore an idea by means of a set of images. But Dylan Thomas does seem here to have touched on the elements I have mentioned, and to have organized them in a way that is not amenable to reason or sequential thought. I don't mean that there is no thought in the poem, but that it brings together ideas in a different way from the way we would employ argument in trying to prove something. Thomas has brought the ideas together in the hope, perhaps, that they will illuminate each other, if not in the certainty that they clarify each other for himself. He once said of these poems that they were the work of a boily boy in love with words and would be understood by another boily boy, or boily girl.

---

[1]The sense of euphoria (described by Freud as the "óceanic feeling", a feeling of being at one with things, of feeling marvellously elated, committed, right, etc) at the moment of creation is for many creative people a narcotic which, when it goes, after the initial process of creation, leaves them despairing and dissatisfied with their work, often feeling it is valueless. For some the anguish of this is almost too great to bear and makes them restless and sometimes anti-social.

[2]*Collected Poems* (Dent)

Thomas was influenced by Blake and Milton, among others—as can perhaps be seen in the word "Abaddon". I think he was also influenced by the dictionary. If you read the section in the dictionary under "A", both "Abaddon" and "agnail" stand out like—well, we'd better avoid the pun. Whether this is so or not doesn't really matter. I am suggesting that both are extraordinary *words* on their own account, in terms both of their sound and of the meaning they hold. "Agnail" is particularly interesting because it has two forms (agnail and hangnail) and is of confused etymology, meaning both a piece of skin, a cuticle, torn, bleeding or swelling at the corner of the nail, and also an iron nail on which things can be hung (or hanged). The potential of the ambiguity for a poet of Thomas's inclination can immediately be seen: bleeding flesh—nails—Christ (connections in "gentleman lay graveward", "cracked from Adam", "gentleman of wounds", "Old cock from nowheres and the heaven's egg", "Scraped at my cradle in a walking word", etc). Abaddon is a Miltonic word and means Apollyon the destroyer, the angel of the bottomless pit—Hell. Therefore, some of the ideas are the torment, the hell, a taste for the ultimate in torn flesh, broken off (as is an agnail from the finger) from the stock of Adam, also in expiation for Adam's sin, etc. These possibilities seem to me latent in the discrete words, and Thomas saw them and brought them together. The poem is an attempt to do something with these and other related meanings, not to weave them into an argument, but to present them for consideration as a painter might do.

I've spent some time over this because for some students it is a thorny obstacle, both to their appreciation of such imagery in poetry and also in their own writing—they are not sure what they are doing, or what they *might* do with their imagery. Often students, delighted with their own new-found abilities to create striking imagery, are content to leave it on the paper, *unformed* so to speak, and proudly acknowledge Thomas as a mentor. I am anxious to point to the organization of relationships and meanings that is going on, even in these early poems, below the surface[1]—something that is sometimes ignored by Thomas's critics. Also I think the discussion may help to illustrate Thomas's comments about his writing, and the sonnet does it relevantly. (I think he wrote much better poems, but the process he is discussing is evident even in this early poem.)

---

[1]It also goes on consciously and deliberately, of course. See Dylan Thomas's letter to Pamela Hansford Johnson, an extract of which appears in the Appendix p 174.

This is what he has to say:

> A poem by myself *needs* a host of images, because its centre is a host of images. I make one image—though 'make' is not the word; I let, perhaps, an image be 'made' emotionally in me and then apply to it what intellectual and critical forces I possess—let it breed another, let that image contradict the first, make, of the third image bred out of the other two together a fourth contradictory image, and let them all, within my imposed formal limits, conflict...[1]

Students might like to work at an image in the way that Thomas suggests—arising out of anything they are interested in or have a feeling about. But notice his comment about applying his intellectual and critical forces. Obviously he means in terms of taste, relevance, richness of relationship, and in terms of the shape and form and structure of the "host of images".

Ted Hughes takes up the point about critical awareness, but in terms of the words chosen. Words are complex things; they are not just pieces of a jigsaw that can be fitted together to make a pattern; they may connect as the pieces of a jigsaw do, interlocking, but they have their own corners, tendrils, nerve-endings, if you like, and this can cause trouble:

> When the words are pouring out, how can you be sure that you don't have one of the side-meanings of the word 'treacle' all stuck up with one of the side-meanings of the word 'feathers' a few words later? In bad poetry this is exactly what happens, the words kill each other. Luckily, you don't have to bother about it so long as you do one thing.
>
> That one thing is, simply imagine what you're writing about. See it and live it. Don't think it up laboriously, as if you were working out mental arithmetic. Just look at it, touch it, smell it, listen to it, turn yourself into it. When you do this, the words look after themselves, like magic.[2]

But Mr Hughes is at some pains to get the order of priorities right; first you need to know what it is you are writing about, to study it and observe it, to saturate yourself in its nature. (He is concerned

---

[1]From a letter to Henry Treece, quoted in T. H. Jones *Dylan Thomas* (Oliver & Boyd)

[2]From "Capturing Animals" in *Poetry in the Making* (Faber)

here particularly with writing about animals.) So, is my suggestion about working with an image to develop it inappropriate? Not if, as the case of Dylan Thomas shows, the image you have is one which interests you, which your imagination has a stake in, so to speak. The two poets are noting different features of the business of using words; their arguments are not mutually exclusive. Mr Hughes is trying to get young people to write out of what they know and can observe rather than in order to satisfy some requirement to write in a "poetic" way, which can only be artificial. And perhaps I ought to say here that a book such as this can be no substitute for the student's interest in the world, ideas, feelings, and language. Its usefulness is, I hope, in that it might draw attention to ideas in which the student may have an interest, and of which the potential may not have been recognized.

John Keats, who was fascinated by the process of the creative imagination, fortunately for us often committed his reflections to paper in the form of letters to his family and friends. Here he talks of what he calls "Negative Capability". He seems to have seen the poetic process as the harnessing of intangibles, the reconciliation of opposites, as Coleridge, pondering on the same thing, referred to it, the business of trying to get into words somehow what is elusive, amorphous in the imagination, that *terra incognita* about which D. H. Lawrence writes (see p 125). However, here is the relevant passage from Keats' letter to Tom and Georgina:

> Several things dovetailed in my mind, and at once it struck me, what quality went to form a Man of Achievement—I mean Negative Capability, that is when a man is capable of being in uncertainties, mysteries, doubts, without any irritable reaching after fact and reason—Coleridge, for instance, would let go by a fine isolated verisimilitude caught from the Penetralium of mystery, from being incapable of remaining content with half knowledge. This pursued through volumes would perhaps take us no further than this, that with a great poet the sense of Beauty overcomes every other consideration, or rather obliterates all considerations.[1]

And typical of Keats that ultimately he identifies the process as "the sense of Beauty", which elsewhere he considered as Truth. Put like

[1]Letter December 27 1817

this, bearing in mind his poems, I think Lawrence might have agreed with him. It is interesting that so often, when you put side by side the comments of writers from different periods, although their words are different and even their avowed aims may be different, their ideas seem to be the same.

T. S. Eliot was also concerned with the difficulties of conveying the elusive features of human emotion[1]: these could be settled on an image of something that stood between the writer and the reader, something chosen by the writer, already invested with a particular meaning to which the writer added by presenting the image in a new context. Eliot called this thing that stood between the writer and the reader the "objective correlative": an image, an idea, a picture, a word which has certain connotations that the reader will recognize or, perhaps, respond to unconsciously. For example, most people familiar with some English Literature will recall the impact of Enobarbus's description of Cleopatra on the river Cydnus in *Antony and Cleopatra:*

> *The barge she sat in, like a burnish'd throne*
> *Burn'd on the water:* etc[2]

So that when Eliot imports the reference to Cleopatra in an ironic context in "The Waste Land", the effect to some extent controls the reader's response. The irony is the greater in that the reference to Cleopatra is coupled with one to Pope's description of Belinda before her mirror in *The Rape of the Lock.* The account of Cleopatra is lush, rich without irony, a glory from a former age; Belinda in her glory is presented by Pope, for the purposes of his satire, in an ambivalent light: she is in ironic contrast with a goddess or high priestess from some earlier classical age ("...decks the Goddess with the glittering spoil..." I, l. 120ff), just as the lady in T. S. Eliot's poem, the contemporary beauty, neurotic, before her mirror, is in ironic contrast with both of them, thus heightening or sharpening the picture Eliot is making:

> *'My nerves are bad tonight. Yes, bad. Stay with me.*
> *Speak to me. Why do you never speak. Speak.*
> *What are you thinking of? What thinking? What?*[3] etc

---

[1]See refs to Langer p 124; also Eliot's lines p 128
[2]Act II sc. ii l. 191 [3]"The Waste Land" (Faber)

The allusions to Cleopatra, Belinda and also, incidentally, to Dido (another glamorous figure from a rich earlier age) connect in the reader's mind and dispose him (if he is sensitive to them, and, of course, if he's familiar with them) to a mode of feeling and understanding that Eliot is trying to evoke in the poem; they act as an "objective correlative":

> The only way of expressing emotion in the form of art is by finding an 'Objective correlative', in other words, a set of objects, a situation, a chain of events which shall be the *formula* of that particular emotion...[1]

Most writers, poets especially, attest the power of the imagination and hold to Blake's view: "One power alone makes a poet: Imagination, the Divine Vision"—the power to recognize and transform, to *re-create*. Characteristically the eighteenth century, following Dryden, saw the whole business in compartmentalized form, but imagination nevertheless came first:

> The first happiness of the poet's imagination is properly invention, or the finding of the thought; the second is fancy or the variation, deriving, or moulding of that thought, as the judgement represents it proper to the subject; the third is elocution, or the art of clothing and adorning that thought, as found and varied in apt, significant, and sounding words; the quickness of the imagination is seen in the invention, the fertility in the fancy, and the accuracy in the expression.[2]

The complexity of the use of images in conjunction is well demonstrated by Coleridge in his comments on two lines from Shakespeare's *Venus and Adonis,* and by I. A. Richards[3] in his comments on what Coleridge had to say:

> *Look! how a bright star shooteth from the sky*
> *So glides he in the night from Venus' eye.*
> *Venus and Adonis* l. 815-16

> How many images and feelings are here brought together without effort and without discord—the beauty of Adonis—the rapidity of his flight—the yearning yet helplessness of the enamoured gazer—and a shadowy ideal character thrown over the whole.
> Coleridge

[1]From *The Sacred Wood* 1927 [2]Dryden Preface to *Annus Mirabilis*
[3]In *Coleridge on Imagination* (Routledge & Kegan Paul)

> ...the more the image is followed up, the more links of relevance between the units are discovered. As Adonis to Venus, so these lines to the reader seem to linger in the eye like the after-images that make the trail of the meteor. Here Shakespeare is realizing, and making the reader realize—not by any intensity of effort, but by the fullness and self-completing growth of the response—Adonis' flight as it was to Venus, and the sense of loss, of increased darkness, that invades her. The separable meanings of each word, *Look!* (our surprise at the meteor, hers at his flight), *star* (a light-giver, an influence, a remote and uncontrollable thing), *shooteth* (the sudden, irremediable, portentous fall to death of what had been a guide, a destiny), *the sky* (the source of light and now of ruin), *glides* (not rapidly only, but with fatal ease too), *in the night* (the darkness of the scene and of Venus' world now)—all these separable meanings are here brought into one. And as they come together, as the reader's mind finds cross-connexion after cross-connexion between them, he seems, in becoming more aware of them, to be discovering not only Shakespeare's meaning, but something which he, the reader, is himself making. His understanding of Shakespeare is sanctioned by his own activity in it. As Coleridge says: 'You feel him to be a poet, inasmuch as for a time he has made you one—an active creative being'.
>
> I. A. Richards

It is a marvellous business, something to wonder at and something obsessive if you once get caught by it. As Eliot says:

> Anyone who has ever been visited by the muse is henceforth haunted...

The following are comments by novelists and playwrights on their craft which students might like to discuss:

> You are now collecting your People delightfully, getting them exactly into such a spot as is the delight of my life:- 3 or 4 Families in a Country Village is the very thing to work on.
>
> Jane Austen Letter to Fanny, 1814

> A novel is an impression, not an argument.
>
> Hardy Preface to Tess of the D'Urbervilles

> We have defined a story as a narrative of events arranged in their time sequence. A plot is also a narrative of events, the emphasis falling on causality. 'The king died and then the queen died,' is a

story. 'The king died, and then the queen died of grief,' is a plot. The time-sequence is preserved, but the sense of causality overshadows it. Or again: 'The queen died, no one knew why, until it was discovered that it was through grief at the death of the king.' This is a plot with a mystery in it, a form capable of high development. It suspends the time sequence, it moves as far away from the story as its limitations will allow. Consider the death of the queen. If it is a story we say: 'And then?' If it is in a plot we ask: 'Why?'. That is the fundamental difference between these two aspects of the novel. A plot cannot be told to a gaping audience of cave men or to a tyrannical sultan or to their modern descendant the movie-public. They can only be kept awake by 'And then—and then—and then—' they can only supply curiosity. But a plot demands intelligence and memory also.

E. M. Forster *Aspects of the Novel*[1]

I always begin with a particular character in a particular dilemma. And then I ask myself what would such a man do in such a situation? What is he really like? What is the nature of the dilemma? And then I work at the novel to find out.

Georges Simenon TV Interview

At first I had a basic idea for a story. I tried to write a novella. Title: *Eclipse of the Moon.* It took place in a mountain village, an emigrant came home from America and took revenge on his old rival. That was the first phase. Then the second: The emigrant turned into a woman, the multibillionairess, Claire Zachanassian. The mountain village became Güllen. Now here I can sketch the play's development more exactly. Dramatically the first problem that came up was this: how can I show a small town on the stage? At that time I was frequently travelling from Neuenburg, where I lived, to Berne. The express train always stops once or twice at little tiny stations. Next to these little buildings there's a small comfort station. It's a very typical sight at a small railway station then; it can be used very well as a stage picture. Now, the railway station is the first place you see when you come into a town, that's where you have to arrive. The spectator comes into Güllen with the railway station, so to speak.

[1]Edward Arnold

Then there was the dramatic problem to solve: how do I represent poverty now? Just letting the people run around in rags, for example, wouldn't be nearly enough; the whole place has to be impoverished. And that's how I got the idea that I'd make a point of not having the express train stop there anymore; it used to stop but not anymore. So the town has sunk. Now there was a further question: how does a billionairess arrive? Does she take a local train? Of course, I could have her come in a special train, but naturally it's more elegant if she pulls the emergency cord. Billionairesses can afford that. But then, I'm having a billionairess come by train, why by train at all? Why didn't she come by car? And here, from this tight spot—since I wanted to have the railway station at all costs as a milieu—I came on the idea that the billionairess is coming by train because she once had an auto accident and now has an artificial leg, and can't drive anymore. You can see from these examples how elements of the play derive from theatrical necessities, concrete necessities of the stage, and just seem to be simple ideas.

Dürrenmatt on *The Visit*[1]

The process goes like this: I discover that I have gotten an idea somewhere. I never *get* an idea—I discover that I have one. Then over the next six months or a year or two years, it gradually, slowly develops—I think about it occasionally. The characters are forming at that time, and eventually after a certain period of time when the idea seems both vague enough and clear enough to start working on, and the characters seem three dimensional enough to carry the burden of work by themselves, then I go to the typewriter. So the actual writing time is very short—anything from a month to three months. But the pre-writing process—which is a form of writing, I suppose—takes a good deal of time...

Edward Albee[2]

SEE also p 59 Virginia Woolf on Modern Fiction; p 68 Harold Pinter on writing for the stage; p 174 Dylan Thomas on integrity in poetry.

[1]and[2]From *The Playwrights Speak* Ed. by Walter Wagner (Longman)

APPENDIX

The rock-pool glowed beneath the glimmering keel of the boat like a quivering emerald, the long ribbons of milky light penetrating it slowly, stealing down like golden probes. About four fathoms, I thought, and drawing a deep breath rolled over and let my body wangle downwards like a fish, not using my arms.

Its beauty was spell-binding. It was like diving into the nave of a cathedral whose stained-glass windows filtered the sunlight through a dozen rainbows. The sides of the amphitheatre—for it opened gradually towards the deep sea—seemed as if carved by some heartsick artist of the Romantic Age into a dozen half-finished galleries lined with statues. Some of these were so like real statuary that I thought for a moment that I had made an archeological find. But these blurred caryatids were wave-born, pressed and moulded by the hazard of the tides into goddesses and dwarfs and clowns. A light marine fucus of brilliant yellow and green had bearded them—shallow curtains of weed which swung lightly in the tide, parting and closing, as if to reveal their secrets suggestively and then cover them again. I pushed my fingers through this scalp of dense and slippery foliage to press them upon the blind face of a Diana or the hooked nose of a medieval dwarf. The floor of this deserted palace was of selenite plastic clay, soft to the touch and in no way greasy. Terracotta baked in a dozen hues of mauve and violet and gold. Inside close to the island it was not deep—perhaps a fathom and a half—but it fell away steeply where the gallery spread out to the sea, and the deeper lining of water faded from emerald to apple green, and from Prussian blue to black, suggesting great depth. Here, too, was the wreck of which Clea had spoken. I had hopes of finding perhaps a Roman amphora or two, but it was not alas a very old ship. I recognized the flared curve of the poop as an Aegean design—the type of caique which the Greeks call '*trechandiri*'. She had been rammed astern. Her back was broken. She was full of a dead weight of dark sponges. I tried to find the painted eyes on the prow and a name, but they had vanished. Her wood was crawling with slime and every cranny winked full of hermit crabs. She must have belonged to sponge fishers of Kalymnos I thought, for each year their fleet crosses to fish the African coast and carry its haul back for processing in the Dodecanese Islands.

A blinding parcel of light struck through the ceiling now and down flashed the eloquent body of Clea, her exploding coils of hair swerved up behind her by the water's concussion, her arms spread. I caught her and we rolled and sideslipped down in each other's arms, playing like fish until lack of breath drove us upwards once more into the sunlight. To sit at last panting in the shallows, gazing with breathless delight at each other.

From *Clea* Lawrence Durrell (Faber)

*

I . . always with I . . one starts from . . one and I share the same character are one . . . . . one always starts with I . . one . . . . . . alone . . . . sole . . . . single I

I have no means of telling, here, down here, when they will shoot, but I do know, the sound reaches me down here, it is one of the few sounds that do reach me down here, when they are going to haul. CRAANGK! It has just gone, once, against the side: they release the towing block aft, it whangs hard against the side, and I know they have started to haul.... Sometimes it wakes me, sometimes more than once during the sixteen hours a day I spend asleep, or spend on my bunk, rather, for the towing block craangks against the stern just above my head: the towing block is just above, up, and outside, of course, right near my head: that is probably why this bunk was free, why the others were not using it, did not want to use it, that I could have it....

Opening of *Trawl* by B. S. Johnson
(Secker & Warburg/Panther Books)

*

AS THE MIRRORS LIE

Slowly, the watchful eyes of Mrs B studied her reflection. Pursing her lips, fat in her pale, scraped face, a mirror-image Mrs B faced the real one. Both remained a long time, wary, calculating, as if ready to pounce; then the pasty lips and cheeks fell slack, the eyes creased in a sudden child-like pouting anger, and the bottle swung from Mrs B's plump hand to hit the mirror with a resounding hellish give of folding glass-silver shards flew, liberated, from the head of Mrs B., and lay, a world of silent smouldering memories and long white-cold days, shattered in an instant on the brown floor. It was...absurd. Mrs. looked, swaying, in the mirror, and a headless, mindless Mrs B. looked, swaying, back. The brown floor came up to meet her.

A sensation. Day.
Night.
Day. Night. Day Night day night day nightdaynightdaynightday

And there was Mrs B., a plump, drunken figure, lying crumpled as a baby on the floor, her eyes on the broken mirror near her head. Mirror mirror on the wall, she mouths silently, awkward as a fish on land. On her head, terribly hot, hot and heavy, like—like boiling seaweed—she let out a laugh that rattled round the room, and lay, panting and giggling into the fragments of glass whitewhite on the brownbrown floor. The mirror faithfully reflected her bare, collapsed face; and the spasm over, Mrs B. lay muddled, emptily regarding the mirrored face that vacantly regarded her. Oh, what a face! she suddenly thought. A foul breath dumped a sudden mist over the tiny face-fragment. Good, oh goodgood she thought, that—face—isn't even mine really. Oh no, no. No. Thoughts began to be in the crazed labyrinth of her mind, breaking, rejoining running like globules of quicksilver, scattering, reforming, sliding loud down the walls of her brain:

Once, she had been a girl, a shining example of blonde beauty, a world away from a fat housewife. She had been perfect of figure and feature; oh, Mrs B., whatever happened! (A silent image of a lipsticked girl in a tight red dress is running like a well-worn cartoon, through the dead dark memories).

She had been pretty, simple, easily drawn away from her neat and timelessly ordered home with many promises of fun, marriage—and many had succeeded (but those memories were taken and pushed right down to the bottom, glossed over with years of drinking, mellowed; people only remember what they want, Mrs. B.) And there was her husband. How had it happened?

One moment a dashing, exciting young man, the next a dreadful changed creature, his face grown bald and impartial, his very presence revolting, all encased in the house like a film: two people enclosed, hemmed in with the sordid reality of life, tables and chairs and washing-up, condemned to aeons of married life while the light-bulbs burnt out their years—Mrs B., oh Mrs B! The face you breathe so viley upon began to form back then. Days and nights of unspeakable ordinariness, thick with hate and monotony, had spread far and wide; had pulled her face down out of shape, pressed and folded the great wads of pasty fat, fixed it in a dull frame of discontent and misery and hate. And now look in the mirror, Mrs B.

She felt sudden whining anger as she lay there, a slack bag of fat, beside the glinting shards. Damn, oh Goddamn, why wouldn't the mirror reflect the girl—the young naive self she had once been? The memory of good days filled her brain.

A shaft of light filtered through the dust in the air. A whimper swelled in the throat of Mrs B. She glimpsed the bottle on the floor and her lips fell into a sudden flabby O. A sigh welled up from her heart and she floundered on the brown floor like a great feeble whale-fish, her little pig-eyes vacant, her mouth panting a foetid breath over the splintered mirror, the brash, clean mirror that refused—refused to re-distort her features, refused to melt them kindly back to her old-young days. Again, the red-dressed image ran, distant, unreal, through her mind.

Pursued by her husband. Husband, husband, the very word was... obscene...oh, she hated her dead (and gone?) husband. He hated her too, oh, when he'd died he'd told her what He thought. With a smooth nightmarish shudder, the room bulged in round Mrs B's dulled senses, and flickered away like a soap bubble: a smile faced her from the rose-patterned wall. Smiling, pretentious, He. The frame held him stamped indelibly, finally, to the prosaic wallpaper. He was permanent, his back hate framed the room, the house, the day and the night. Grunting like a sow, Mrs B. aimed an oddly detached yet heavy hand at the luridly grinning face. She watched the thing jar, fall slowly turn once—incredible, stupid as a joke—in the air, then lie, defeated: when she picked it up, glass fell out onto the floor.

Faces, faces, but never the one she wanted to see. He hated her that was why, he could not bear her gross presence; were she suddenly to change back to a twenty-one year old, she thought he would have liked her even less: oh life was so unfair, unjust, oh so bad. Better—better drunk than sober.

Thus the pattern of her days and nights: better drunk than sober, trying to forget yet hanker back to her former halcyon days (and surely they were halcyon? You only remember what you want to, Mrs B. remember that.) Days and nights freed to some extent by the bottle, while she became drunk, useless, a misshapen hulk, old, sweating sheer blind incalculable shuddering hate, and shouldering a dull awareness of her future, stretching before her, endless brownbrown floors and untruthful white-glaring mirrors. THE MIRRORS LIE! she thought, they steal your reflection and send it twinkling back, ugly, bad, foully breathing with Him behind you, over you, around you, an invisible thread of triumphant hate that binds the days together. Oh Mrs B!

Time passed. That sudden thought black-lettered itself in her mind. The Mirrors Lie! She fed the idea as it grew and blossomed. Why wouldn't the mirrors show what she wanted them to? It—it was her husband, she thought grimly. He controls the mirrors in this house so they reflect what the onlooker hates most. A vision of fat and a pale, shadowed face swam up at her from the depths of another mirror. God, there were mirrors all around in this house! And one of them was smashed where the head should have been: Oh! Mirrors, reflections, light drawing out rainbows from the cut-glass, rainbows that slanted from the mirrors too in a mockery of what beauty lay behind the glass, concealed—and yet they reflected her! So fat, a slobbering bulk, a drunken idiot, obsessed—obsessedobsessed with

THE MIRRORS THAT LIE
THE MIRRORS THAT LIE.

The evening was slowly draining the afternoon when Mrs B. stood heavy with the bottle clutched in her right hand. Outside, the sun burnt like a brassy plaque, the wrong colour, too bright yet cold for evening. Mrs B. stood dreamily, swaying very slightly. Outside, clouds gathered, black on the pink horizon. The sun burnt itself briefly out and began to slip, defeated, down the sky. A darkening.

Sun/Cloud, Sun eclipsed! The brilliant round dropped, final as a curse, into the menacing clouds that squatted malevolent on the line of the hill. Storm! STORM! The clouds heaved and broiled as the sky fell dark, stolen of its sun. Time hung heavy, awful, with aeons meeting where Mrs B. stood in the middle of the floor, and all heaven emptied dark and nightmare clouds chased alive across the void above, cold winds threw the curtains a-flapping, stricken like old lavender-bag ladies at the window.—Mrs B. stood, and while the rain wet the ground silently, then drumming fiercer through the terrified air, she dreamt of the thought shining beacon-like in the growing murk of the room and her mind. Her old self! She had to find her old self!! The mirrors, she reasoned muzzily. The mirrors must be made not to lie! A cat ran howling across the street below. The air vibrated, tense as a plucked string; it quivered, agonised, as the rain poured, pummelled, dripped and, flowed; Mrs B. thought! The air streamed and winds banged about the houses to disappear, soaring aloft to the bullying, staring clouds. Her old self! Where? Where was she!?

Deep below the saturated street, dust lifted in the dry drains and swirled away on eddies of heaven-water—The mirrors must be found, and shown,—and the weather screamed and terrified the world and became stronger and wetter and a flash of brilliant lightning briefly illuminated Mrs B's moving back as she climbed the stairs.

Her feet guided her into grey rain-made darkness, shadowed passageways; sudden menacing doors she passed, eyes fixed ahead, half her mind frozen with fear, longing to run in panic and hide hide far away look away cold rigid beating heart in smallest safest place but oh! The image of her old self ballooned, drew itself up, filled her mind, oozed like the subterranean rain through its dark labyrinth, filled it to plenitude.

As if in a dream, a dumpy woman with a dark green mind plods and presses on and on through the awful house. Lightning! A sudden flash stirred her fear, but, as if mesmerised by the image of her once-lovely self, the figure walks on.

The lightning flashes round her. Her mind cannot think any more, and the image—the smile, the blonde hair, the pert nose—it eats her until she passes along the passage like a heavy husk —

The door of her room looms soft, gaping, ahead. Beyond, in that darkness filled with the enticing sound of rain falling, falling like emotion past emotion, the mirror glimmers gently.

Not a movement, not the smallest twitch or flutter of an eyelash Mrs B. stands, stoic yet strangely impersonal, floating, like the house floats in the endless rain outside.

Suspended silence with the dark green brain pausing on the threshold of the momentous room. Stillness.

Quietude.

Then suddenly deep inside the mirror, the one smashed where the head should have been, a movement flashed that awoke the heaving silence: a million mirrors flashed back in Mrs B's head, and she walked forward, toward the node of light, of life. There was a thought, now churning, now still, in her mind—it concerned a red-dressed image that ran, quick as habit, echoing through her brain, and He, and power, and surely she would show He was no master here! Her face was greyly lit in the grey rainlight. A far-off, unreal flash of lightning quickly hurled the room into light and as quickly smashed it back to darkness again.

Mrs B. walked the acres of darkness into the gently breathing box of the room, her feet plodding slowly on, her eyes bulging in their sockets.

Triumphantly, she neared the mirror (all the time the space before her) and finally stood, eyes closed, puffy face tense, grotesque eyelids twitched shut over the fixed silent eyes. (Outside the rain drummed its knuckles over all, and water ran streaming from its fingers, and there was Mrs B. in the drowned room, the dust of the mantel parched as a mummy.) Somewhere in a dark room in a stormy town a fat woman emits a tiny gurgling sigh and opens her eyes...

There was a woman in the mirror a headless image, because

Mrs B. stood, chuckling like an idiot, eyebrows twitching, mouth a dribbling hole in her death-white pasty face: still the eyes stared unblinking yet satiated, supremely victorious, at the red dress in the mirror before her.

Headless, unutterably grotesque, the imagebody began to sway, dip, allure. The smooth shapely legs took one tiny step back, and an arm flashed whitely across, beckoning, dreamlike, the dream of an old woman, terrible, beautiful. Pity about the face, thought Mrs B., terrifyingly coherent behind her own; and as the tall rain runnelled noisily down the middle of the road far away outside, there in her room stood a fat woman before a liquid, beckoning image. (That's shown him, she thought complacently.) The huge body began to shake with dry laughter that fell breathily from her fat lips and vanished into the soft blackness. A presence seemed to be all around her. The memory of her husband stood like a bat at the door, beat fierce with hate about her ears, and lay in a smouldering puddle at her feet—and the mirror shimmered and beckoned. Hate, the filthy hate of years, grew round her shoulders and crept, like the scum of water now covering the street, from the four corners of the room: Mrs B. stood, paunchy, and listened. No sound but the rain and a faint crackling of the gathering hate about her, her husband's dry laugh dwindled and folded to an elfin tinyness but as full of hate as ever.

Certain, sure for the first time in her life, Mrs B. stepped delicately forward, slowly, oh, so slowly. Cocking her head like a gross misshapen bird, she pursed her lips and stepped once more. Slowly

silently she

fell through the rushing air in a perfect arc,

obscenely huge,

straight into the mirror

to join her image and escape Him.

Behind the frail wall of glass the certain Mrs B. came to rest. And looked up, composed, at her old self.

A million tiny shards flew from the face of the red-dressed girl before her and lay, shattered, dead whitewhite on the brownbrown floor! A bald man of (perhaps) forty looked from the place where the head should have been, triumphant, his laugh an elfin crackling that grew and gathered strength with the seconds.

Mrs B. knelt, petrified, and her eyes grew tears that dripped and runnelled from her weeping distracted eyes, and her mouth blubbered stupid words of mercy oh God! God! Her HUSBAND IN THE MIRROR, the memories had all gone wrong, oh with all hell before in fire and flame she whimpered,

THE MIRRORS LIE

eyes stare THE MIRRORS LIE
she crumples THE MIRRORS

And only a man trudging cold through the rain on the street below heard a terrible, last scream and saw the same flash of lightning that illuminated, for one mind-shattering instant, a devastated woman lying dead before a mirror that reflected the head of a man, staring and laughing.

On the street below, a lone man disappeared into the rain.

Rosemary Kathleen Chandler, aged 16
In *Daily Mirror Children as Writers 4* (Heinemann)

*

She stood before the mirror and she was afraid. It was the summer of fear, for Frankie, and there was one fear that could be figured in arithmetic with paper and pencil at the table. This August she was twelve and five-sixths old. She was five feet five and three-quarter inches tall, and she wore a number seven shoe. In the past year she had grown four inches, or at least that was what she judged. Already the hateful little summer children hollered to her: 'Is it cold up there?' And the comments of grown people made Frankie shrivel on her heels. If she reached her height on her eighteenth birthday, she had five and one-sixth growing years ahead of her. Therefore, according to mathematics and unless she could somehow stop herself, she would grow to be over nine feet tall. And what would be a lady who is over nine feet high? She would be a Freak.

Carson McCullers
From *The Member of the Wedding* (Cresset Press/Penguin)

*

Yeats' "Byzantium"
The poem and first drafts

The unpurged images of day recede;
The Emperor's drunken soldiery are abed;
Night resonance recedes, night-walkers' song
After great cathedral gong;
A starlit or a moonlight dome disdains
All that man is,
All mere complexities,
The fury and the mire of human veins.

Before me floats an image, man or shade,
Shade more than man, more image than a shade;
For Hades' bobbin bound in mummy-cloth
May unwind the winding path;
A mouth that has no moisture and no breath
Breathless mouths may summon;
I hail the superhuman;
I call it death-in-life and life-in-death.

Miracle, bird or golden handiwork,
More miracle than bird or handiwork,
Planted on the star-lit golden bough,
Can like the cocks of Hades crow,
Or, by the moon embittered, scorn aloud
In glory of changeless metal
Common bird or petal
And all complexities of mire or blood.

At midnight on the Emperor's pavement flit
Flames that no faggot feeds, nor steel has lit,
Nor storm disturbs, flames begotten of flame,
Where blood-begotten spirits come
And all complexities of fury leave,
Dying into a dance,
An agony of trance,
An agony of flame that cannot singe a sleeve.

Astraddle on the dolphin's mire and blood,
Spirit after spirit! The smithies break the flood,
The golden smithies of the Emperor!
Marbles of the dancing floor
Break bitter furies of complexity,
Those images that yet
Fresh images beget,
That dolphin-torn, that gong-tormented sea.

Early note for the poem:

Subject for a poem

Describe Byzantium as it is in the system towards the end of the first Christian millenium. ~~The worn ascetics on the walls contrasted with their (?) splendour. A walking mummy. A spiritual refinement and perfection~~ amid a rigid world. ~~A sigh of wind autumn leaves in the streets. The divine born amidst natural decay.~~

Over cancelled lines he then wrote:

A walking mummy; flames at the street corners where the soul is purified. Bird of hammered gold singing in the golden trees. In the harbour (dolphins) offering their backs to the wailing dead that they may carry them to paradise. These subjects have been in my head for some time, especially the last.

First draft:

When (______) all
~~When all that roaring rout of rascals (   ) are a bed~~
~~When every roaring rascal is a bed~~
~~When the last brawler's tumbled into bed,~~
~~When the emperor's brawling soldiers are bed~~
~~When the last brawler tumbles into bed~~

When the emperor's brawling soldiers are abed
~~When the last~~
~~When the last~~
~~The last robber~~
~~The last benighted robber or army fled~~
~~When the last~~
~~The last robber or his~~
thieves' last benighted traveller
The ~~night thieves' latest victim~~ dead or fled
~~Silence fallen~~
When
~~When starlit purple~~
~~beats down~~
~~When~~ death like ~~sleep has destroys the harlot's song~~

~~And the great cathedral gong~~
~~When~~

And silence falls on the cathedral gong
And the drunken harlot's song

Then he collects the salvaged lines:

When the emperor's brawling soldiers are a bed
The last benighted victim dead or fled;
When
~~And~~ silence falls on the cathedral gong
And the drunken harlot's song
a
~~On~~ cloudy silence, or a silence lit
Whether by star or moon
I tread the emperor's town,
All my intricacies grown clear & sweet

And so on through thirteen pages.

These items are taken from Jon Stallworthy's book *Between the Lines,* (Oxford) a fascinating account of Yeats' poetry in the making. In the book Stallworthy follows the development of this and other poems through all the stages of their composition, sometimes from a single idea, to the finished poem.

*

Her hands on the keyboard. Pale hands with thin fingers, and very short nails. On Sundays she wears white gloves: when they walk back from church he takes her hand. He is fascinated by an old fascination: her fingers touch the keys in two very different ways. Either they touch them so lightly that no sooner have they touched them than they desist and fly on; or else they descend heavily upon them, pressing the keys down and keeping them down, so that he can see the unpolished sides of the adjacent keys. It is then as though she forces her fingers through the piano. The last note dies away.

From the novel *G* by John Berger
(Weidenfeld & Nicolson/Penguin)

*

THE LEGS

There was this road,
And it led up-hill,
And it led down-hill,
And round and in and out.

And the traffic was legs,
Legs from the knees down,
Coming and going,
Never pausing.

And the gutters gurgled
With the rain's overflow,
And the sticks on the pavement
Blindly tapped and tapped.

What drew the legs along
Was the never-stopping,
And the senseless, frightening
Fate of being legs.

Legs for the road,
The road for legs,
Resolutely nowhere
In both directions.

My legs at least
Were not in that rout:
On grass by the roadside
Entire I stood,

Watching the unstoppable
Legs go by
With never a stumble
Between step and step.

Though my smile was broad
The legs could not see,
Though my laugh was loud
And legs could not hear.

My head dizzied, then:
I wondered suddenly,
Might I too be a walker
From the knees down?

Gently I touched my shins.
The doubt unchained them:
They had run in twenty puddles
Before I regained them.

Robert Graves *Collected Poems* (Cassell)

*

WELSH INCIDENT

'But that was nothing to what things came out
From the sea-caves of Criccieth yonder.'
'What were they? Mermaids? dragons? ghosts?'
'Nothing at all of any things like that.'
'What were they, then?'
'All sorts of queer things.
Things never seen or heard or written about,
Very strange, un-Welsh, utterly peculiar
Things. Oh, solid enough they seemed to touch,
Had anyone dared it. Marvellous creation,
All various shapes and sizes and no sizes,
All new, each perfectly unlike his neighbour,
Though all came moving slowly out together.'
'Describe just one of them.'
'I am unable.'
'What were their colours?'
'Mostly nameless colours,
Colours you'd like to see; but one was puce
Or perhaps more like crimson, but not purplish.
Some had no colour.'
'Tell me, had they legs?'
'Not a leg nor foot among them that I saw.'
'But did these things come out in any order?
What o'clock was it? What was the day of the week?
Who else was present? How was the weather?'
'I was coming to that. It was half-past three
On Easter Tuesday last. The sun was shining.
The Harlech Silver Band played *Marchog Jesu*
On thirty-seven shimmering instruments,
Collecting for Carnarvon's (Fever) Hospital Fund.
The population of Pwllheli, Criccieth,
Portmadoc, Borth, Tremadoc, Penrhyndeudraeth,
Were all assembled. Criccieth's mayor addressed them

First in good Welsh and then in fluent English,
Twisting his fingers in his chains of office,
Welcoming the things. They came out on the sand,
Not keeping time to the band, moving seaward
Silently at a snail's pace. But at last
The most odd, indescribable thing of all,
Which hardly one man there could see for wonder
Did something recognizably a something.'
'Well, what?'

'It made a noise.'

'A frightening noise?'

'No, no.'

'A musical noise? A noise of scuffling?'

'No, but a very loud, respectable noise—
Like groaning to oneself on Sunday morning
In Chapel, close before the second psalm.'
'What did the mayor do?'

'I was coming to that.'

Robert Graves *Collected Poems* (Cassell)

*

Every definite image in the mind is steeped and dyed in the free water that flows around it. The significance, the value of the image is all in this halo or penumbra that surrounds and escorts it....Consciousness does not appear to itself chopped up in bits....It is nothing jointed; it flows....Let us call it the stream of thought, of consciousness, or of subjective life.

William James "Principles of Psychology" 1890

*

SWANN'S WAY

For a long time I used to go to bed early. Sometimes, when I had put out my candle, my eyes would close so quickly that I had not even time to say "I'm going to sleep". And half an hour later the thought that it was time to go to sleep would awaken me; I would try to put away the book which, I imagined, was still in my hands, and to blow out the light; I had been thinking all the time, while I was asleep, of what I had just been reading, but my thoughts had run into a channel of their own, until I myself seemed actually to have become the subject of my book: a church, a quartet, the rivalry between Francois I and Charles V. This impression would persist for some moments after I was awake; it did not disturb my mind, but it lay like scales upon my eyes and prevented them from registering the fact that the candle was no longer burning. Then it would begin to seem unintelligible, as the thoughts of a former existence must be to a reincarnate spirit; the subject of my book would separate itself from me, leaving me free to choose whether I would form part of it or no; and at the same time my sight would return and I would be astonished to find myself in a state of darkness, pleasant and restful enough for the eyes, and even more, perhaps, for my mind, to which it appeared incomprehensible, without a cause, a matter dark indeed.

I would ask myself what o'clock it could be; I could hear the whistling of trains, which, now nearer and now farther off, punctuating the distance like the note of a bird in a forest, showed me in perspective the deserted countryside through which a traveller would be hurrying towards the nearest station: the path that he followed being fixed for ever in his memory by the general excitement due to being in a strange place, to doing unusual things, to the last words of conversation, to farewells exchanged beneath an unfamiliar lamp which echoed still in his ears amid the silence of the night; and to the delightful prospect of being once again at home.

I would lay my cheeks gently against the comfortable cheeks of my pillow, as plump and blooming as the cheeks of babyhood. Or I would strike a match to look at my watch. Nearly midnight. The hour when an invalid, who has been obliged to start on a journey and to sleep in a strange hotel, awakens in a moment of illness and sees with glad relief a streak of daylight shewing under his bedroom door. Oh, joy of joys! it is morning. The servants will be about in a minute: he can ring, and some one will come to look after him. The thought of being made comfortable gives him strength to endure his pain. He is certain he heard footsteps: they come nearer, and then die away. The ray of light beneath his door is extinguished. It is midnight; some one has turned out the gas; the last servant has gone to bed, and he must lie all night in agony with no one to bring him any help.

I would fall asleep, and often I would awake again for short snatches only, just long enough to hear the regular creaking of the wainscot, or to open my eyes to settle the shifting kaleidoscope of the darkness, to savour, in an instantaneous flash of perception, the sleep which lay heavy upon the furniture, the room, the whole surroundings of which I formed but an insignificant part and whose unconsciousness I should very soon return to share. Or, perhaps, while I was asleep, I had returned without the least effort to an earlier stage in my life, now for ever outgrown; and had come under the thrall of one of my childish terrors, such as that old terror of my great-uncle's pulling my curls, which was effectually dispelled on the day—the dawn of a new era to me—on which they were finally cropped from my head. I had forgotten that event during my sleep; I remembered it again immediately I had succeeded in making myself wake up to escape my great-uncle's fingers; still, as a measure of precaution, I would bury the whole of my head in the pillow before returning to the world of dreams.

Opening of *Swann's Way* by Marcel Proust, translated by C. K. Scott-Moncrieff (Chatto & Windus)

*

AN ORDINARY DAY

I took my mind a walk
Or my mind took me a walk—
Whichever was the truth of it.

The light glittered on the water
Or the water glittered in the light.
Cormorants stood on a tidal rock

With their wings spread out,
Stopping no traffic. Various ducks
Shilly-shallied here and there

On the shilly-shallying water.
An occasional gull yelped. Small flowers
Were doing their level best

To bring to the kerb bees like
Aerial charabancs. Long weeds in the clear
Water did Eastern dances, unregarded

By shoals of darning needles. A cow
Started a moo but thought
Better of it... And my feet took me home

And my mind observed to me,
Or I to it, how ordinary
Extraordinary things are or

How extraordinary ordinary
Things are, like the nature of the mind
And the process of observing.

Norman MacCaig
In *Surroundings* (Hogarth Press)

*

A young lady was standing on the steps of one of those brown brick houses which seem the very incarnation of Irish paralysis. A young gentleman was leaning on the rusty railings of the area. Stephen as he passed on his quest heard the following fragment of colloquy out of which he received an impression keen enough to afflict his sensitiveness very severely.

The Young Lady—(drawling discreetly) . . . O, yes . . . I was . . . at the . . . cha . . . pel . . .
The Young Gentleman—(inaudibly) . . . I . . . (again inaudibly) . . . I . . .
The Young Lady—(softly) . . . O . . . but you're . . . ve . . . ry . . . wick . . . ed . . .

This triviality made him think of collecting many such moments in a book of epiphanies. By an epiphany he meant a sudden spiritual manifestation, whether in vulgarity of speech or of gesture or in a memorable phrase of the mind itself. He believed that it was for the man of letters to record these epiphanies with extreme care, seeing that they themselves are the most delicate and evanescent of moments.

James Joyce from *Stephen Hero* (Jonathan Cape), the first version of *A Portrait of the Artist as a Young Man*

*

IT'S RAINING

it is raining women's voices as if they were dead even in memory

you also are raining down marvellous encounters of my life o little drops

and these rearing clouds are beginning to whinny a whole world of auricular

listen to it rain while regret and disdain weep an old fashioned music

listen to the fall of all the perpendiculars of your existence

Guillaume Apollinaire

Comments on Blake's "The Sick Rose" by F. R. Leavis:

To call a rose 'sick' is to make it at once something more than a thing seen. 'Rose' as developed by 'thy bed of crimson joy' evokes rich passion, sensuality at once glowing, delicate and fragrant, and exquisite health. 'Bed of crimson joy' is voluptuously tactual in suggestion, and, in ways we needn't try and analyse, more than tactual—we feel ourselves 'bedding down' in the Rose, and there is also a suggestion of a secret heart ('found out'), the focus of life, down there at the core of the closely clustered and enclosing petals.

The invisible worm,
That flies in the night,
In the howling storm,

Offering its shock of contrast to the warm security of love ('She is all States, and all Princes, I, Nothing else is') conveys the ungovernable otherness of the dark forces of the psyche when they manifest themselves as disharmonies. The poem, we can see, registers a profound observation of a kind we may find developed in many places in D. H. Lawrence—an observation regarding the possessive element there may be in 'love'.

Scrutiny (Cambridge University Press)

*

Extract from a Letter to Pamela Hansford Johnson

A thing I have always noticed and always admired in your verses and poems is the directness of the opening lines; there is never any beating about; you say what you have to say as quickly and as simply as possible. And you have never—as you said of me—put anything in simply to make it more difficult. The 'Poem' is so simple in thought and structure that it loses rather than gains by the repetition of the statement of your alliance of things as diverse as a swallow and a sod. 'Sod' when it rhymes with 'god' is, in itself, a most horrible cliché; whenever I see 'God' in line two of a bad poem I will inevitably look down to line four to see how the poor old sod is dragged in there. And although this is not altogether a bad poem the too-close proximity of 'God', 'sod', 'heifer' & 'zephyr' must lead one to believe that the thought in which these words appear was dictated by the rhymes, and is therefore false. You started off with a very simple thought (I, for one, will never believe that the most valuable thoughts are, of necessity, simple); you confessed that you were one with the 'sparrow', and then, as a natural conclusion, went on to say that you were one with the 'arrow', too. If it comes to that you can say you are one with the barrow as well. For you are, my dear, you certainly are. I'm not trying to be flippant; I'm merely trying to show you, by any method, how *essentially* false such writing is.

I am one with the wind and one with the breezes,
And one with the torrent that drowns the plain,
I am one with the streams and one with the seas-es.
And one with the maggot that snores in the grain.

A rhyming dictionary, a little selection of natural objects, and a halfpenny gift for stringing pretty words together, and one can write like this all day. 'My blood is drawn from the veins of the roses' is on an altogether different plane; here you have added to the by-now meaningless repetition of association, and have contributed something quite lovely both to yourself and to the rose. Is this clear? It's something I'm always hammering at. The man who said, for the first time, *'I see a rose',* said nothing,but the man who said for the first time *'The rose sees me'* uttered a very wonderful truth. There's little value in going on indefinitely saying,

'I am one with the steamship & one with the trolley,
And one with the airdale & one with the collie';

there's too much 'Uncle Tom Collie & all' about that. Primarily, you see the reader refuses to believe that *you* believe you are one with all these things; you have to prove it to him, and you most certainly won't by cataloguing a number of things to which you *say* you are related.

By the magic of words and images you must make it clear to him that the relationships are real. And only in, 'My blood is drawn from the veins of the roses', do you provide any proof. You gave the rose a human vein, and you gave your own vein the blood of the rose; now that *is* relationship. 'I am his son' means little compared with 'I am his flesh and blood'.

This is a final compression of what I want to say about the 'Poem', and what I do want you to read. As it is, the 16 lines are all separate, too separate; you could have written one, gone to sleep, woken up and written the next. Though you talk all through of the relationship of yourself to other things, there is no relationship at all in the poem between the things you example. If you are one with the swallow & one with the rose, then the rose is one with the swallow. Link together these things you talk of, in your words and images, how your flesh covers the tree & the tree's flesh covers you. I see what you have done, of course—'I am one with the opposites', you say. You are, I know, but you must prove it to me by linking yourself to the opposites and by linking the opposites together. Only in the 'rose' line did you do it.

Is this all clear, or am I talking through my new black hat?

From Dylan Thomas
Selected Letters Ed Fitzgibbon (Dent)

*

IMAGO

From the Italian lady
a rich plush cloth
overstitched with gold.

Behind the eye melanous as the cloth,
her hair straight pulled back,
wide eyes overspilling dark seas
she would always travel on,
the anguish of some lost
or slipping love.

The dress heavy as the past
with intricacies
of mat black lace
to the foot poised—
a small grace

she drifts across the widow-walking
stillness of the long-ago room.

And faded voices faintly overheard
at the rim of silence
in the quiet shadow room
of a late afternoon
talking like the ghost-people
behind frosted glass
shapes of their sound beyond the touch
of sense in or out of that otherness.

The talk goes on
the other side of silence—
my grandmother's voice
as she sits and looks
twinkling eyes and beads,
or just combing,
drawing out the threads—
long white hair
smooth as a girl's
in the fireglow.

The brush moves gently,
the only sound under the fire,
the occasional rain outside.
The inadvertent imago
fluttered out of time
flowers
like the recurring rose.

Paddy Kinsale

*

THE THING MADE REAL

The thing made real by
a sudden twist of the mind:
relate the darkness to a face
rather than
impose a face on the darkness
which has no face, in reality.

The Daisy made recognisable
suddenly
by a flash of
magic light, the tongue
of fire, Pentecost.

The ox made real
in its own essence
without change or pollution...
waking up in the cellar to find
him, rusty and contemplative, staring
me in the face
...the thing in its own essence
outside the confines of those
perfunctory fields, in the unlimited
environment of the imagination –
till it thunders into
the consciousness
in all its pure & beautiful
absurdity
like a White Rhinoceros.

Ron Loewinsohn From *Watermelons*
(LeRoi Jones Totem Press)

*

CHAUCER

Women ben full of Ragerie,
Yet swinken nat sans Secresie.
Thilke moral shall ye understond,
From Schoole-boy's Tale of fayre *Irelond:*
Which to the Fennes hath him betake,
To filch the gray Ducke fro the Lake.
Right then, there passen by the Way
His Aunt, and eke her Daughters tway.
Ducke in his Trowzes hath he hent,
Not to be spied of Ladies gent.
'But ho! our Nephew,' (crieth one,)
'Ho!' quoth another, 'Cozen *John*!'
And stoppen, and lough, and callen out,—
This sely Clerk full low doth lout:
They asken that, and talken this,
'Lo here is Coz, and here is Miss.'
But, as he glozeth with Speeches soote,
The Ducke sore tickleth his Erse Roote;
Fore-piece and buttons all-to-brest;
Forth thrust a white Neck, and red Crest.
'*Te-he*,' cry'd Ladies; Clerke nought spake:
Miss star'd; and gray Ducke crieth *Quaake*,
'O Moder, Moder,' (quoth the Daughter,)
'Be thilke same Thing Maids longen a'ter?
Bette is to pyne on Coals and Chalke,
Then trust on Mon, whose yerde can *talke*.'

Alexander Pope

*

Sweeney in Articulo
THE VOICE OF SWEENEY

Sunday is the dullest day, treating
Laughter as a profane sound, mixing
Worship and despair, killing
New thought with dead forms.
Weekdays give us hope, tempering
Work with reviving play, promising
A future life within this one.
Thirst overtook us, conjured up by Budweisserbrau
On a neon sign: we counted our dollar bills.
Then out into the night air, into Maloney's Bar.
And drank whiskey, and yarned by the hour.
Das Herz ist gestorben,* swell dame, echt Bronx.
And when we were out on bail, staying with the Dalai Lama,
My uncle, he gave me a ride on a yak,
And I was speechless. He said, Mamie,
Mamie, grasp his ears. And off we went
Beyond Yonkers, then I felt safe.
I drink most of the year and then I have a Vichy.

Where do we go from here, where do we go,
Out of the broken bottles? Pious sot!
You have no guide or clue for you know only
Puce snakes and violet mastodons, where the brain beats,
And a seltzer is no answer, a vomit no relief,
And the parched tongue no feel of water. Only
There is balm in this YMCA
(Claim now the balm inside the YMCA)
And you will see that there is more in life than
Those vigils at the doors of pubs in the morning,
Or bootings from the doors of pubs at closing time.
I will show you fear in a pile of half-bricks.
  Wer reitet so spät
  Durch Nacht und Wind?
  Es ist der Vater mit seinem Kind.**

'You called me "Baby Doll" a year ago;
You said that I was very nice to know.'
But when we came back late from that Wimbledon dance-hall,
Your arms limp, your hair awry, you could not

Speak, and I likewise, we were neither
Living nor dead, and we knew nothing,
Gazing blankly before us in the carriage.
'Bank Station! All change! Heraus! Heraus!'

Victor Purcell
In *Yet More Comic & Curious Verse* (Penguin)

* Schiller, "Des Mädchens Klange"
**Goethe, "Erlkönig"

LAST WORDS

Much writing is playing with ideas which, nibbling away at the raw edges of the mind, seem to need words and other ideas to feed on. For most of us language is what we feed the ideas on, so that they can grow and find some external shape as a communication with others, but also as an aid to understanding ourselves. Not all of us are likely to desire or be able to make a living out of writing, but I think all of us want to try to understand our experience. This book is intended to promote that activity, to make young people more aware of themselves in relation to the world and people about them, and to help them to use the verbal means that may be latent within them. It's not intended that the book will teach them to write, but it is hoped that they will find a lot of pleasure in trying and might be lured into an activity they are inclined to tackle only with reluctance or even distaste. If it does this in only a tiny measure it will have been enormously successful.

BOOKLIST

Referred to in the text or which students and teacher will find helpful:

BOOKS ABOUT WRITING

Ted Hughes *Poetry in the Making* (Faber)
Robin Skelton *The Practice of Poetry* (Heinemann), *The Poet's Calling* (Heinemann)
Eileen MacKinlay *The Shared Experience* (Methuen)
Poole and Shepherd *Impact I & II & Teachers' Book* (Heinemann)

CONCERNED WITH LITERATURE

D. W. Harding *Experience into Words* (Peregrine)

STORIES

Moffett and McElheny *Points of View* (Mentor)
(Anthology of short stories arranged according to viewpoint of the narrator)

NOTEBOOKS

Gerard Manley Hopkins *Selected Poems and Prose* (Penguin)
(Including extracts from his notebooks).

NOVELS

Obviously there are dozens one might suggest but for a number of reasons the following are important:
James Joyce *Ulysses* (Penguin)
Lawrence Durrell *The Alexandrian Quartet* (Faber)
Patrick White *The Eye of the Storm* (Penguin)
Saul Bellow *Herzog* (Penguin)
John Berger *G* (Penguin)
Samuel Beckett *Malone Dies* (Penguin)
William Golding *Pincher Martin* (Faber)

PHILOSOPHY, PSYCHOLOGY, IMAGINATION

Susanne Langer *Philosophy in a New Key* (Signet)
Peter McKeller *Imagination and Thinking* (Cohen & West)
Brewster Gheslin *The Process of Creation* (Mentor)

GENERAL INDEX

Page numbers in **bold type** indicate major entries

INDEX OF AUTHORS CITED

*indicates young writer
Bold type indicates quotation

THEMATIC INDEX

Entries in **bold type** indicate wider references in the General Index

IMMEDIATE EXPERIENCE (Everyday, commonplace, 'ordinary', etc)

EXOTIC EXPERIENCE (Remote, unusual, adventurous, "second-hand")

STORY WRITING

NOVEL WRITING

PLAY-WRITING

POETRY WRITING

TECHNIQUES (Writers' tricks, Matters of form and patterning, writers' preoccupations, etc.)

THEORY (The creative process, nature of the imagination, etc.)